GOAL SETTING *in the* WRITING CLASSROOM

GOAL SETTING *in the* WRITING CLASSROOM

Building Student Agency, Independence, and Success

Valerie Bolling

Routledge
Taylor & Francis Group
NEW YORK AND LONDON

A Stenhouse Book

Designed cover image: © Getty Images

First published 2026
by Routledge
605 Third Avenue, New York, NY 10158

and by Routledge
4 Park Square, Milton Park, Abingdon, Oxon, OX14 4RN

Routledge is an imprint of the Taylor & Francis Group, an informa business

ISBN: 9781032862231 (pbk)
ISBN: 9781003531869 (ebk)

DOI: 10.4324/9781003531869

Typeset in Garamond Premier Pro
by KnowledgeWorks Global Ltd.

Access the Support Material: www.routledge.com/9781032862231

For the teachers who've achieved their goals and for those who are working hard to achieve them. For the teachers who write alongside their students and for those who may, after reading this book, commit to writing more. And for the teachers who teach all types of students, inspiring them to achieve their goals and flourish as writers and humans. This book is for you.

CONTENTS

ACKNOWLEDGMENTS

Writing is usually considered a solitary act, but bringing a book to fruition is a collaborative effort. *Goal Setting in the Writing Classroom* would not exist without the help of my writing village, and I'm grateful to each person mentioned here.

First, I have to recognize my editor, Kassia Omohundro Wedekind. After seeing me present on a panel at the National Council of Teachers of English (NCTE) annual conference, Kassia emailed me to see if I'd be interested in writing a book for teachers. After careful consideration, I decided to accept the challenge. Having only published children's books before, I was hesitant, but Kassia assured me that she would be a collaborator throughout the process, and she kept her word. Each step of the way she was there. Throughout all stages of the process, we hopped on calls with each other, emailed back-and-forth, and even shared updates about our personal lives. As a result of our frequent communication, Kassia has become a dear friend. I am so appreciative of her belief in me and in this book.

Another person who always believes in me and supports my entire author career is my agent extraordinaire, James McGowan. When I doubted, at the beginning, if I could write this book, James shared that he had no doubt that I would be able to do this. As usual, James was right.

Lindsey Aduskevich is my faithful writing partner. Like James, she supports all of my writing efforts. She consistently serves as an accountability partner, critique partner, and cheerleader.

My husband, Sheldon, says that he's my biggest fan, and I'm so glad that he proclaims that role. He is with me throughout every step of my writing process and supports my endeavors and "author life," even when it infringes upon some of our personal time together. As a teacher himself, Sheldon believed I could write this book and said, "This book is a perfect fit for you because it taps into your experience and skills as an instructional coach, teacher, and writer."

I have a writing community for my children's books, but I had to call upon a different group of people for support with this book. When I reached out to

Melissa Stewart, Kirsten W. Larson, Stephen Briseño, JoEllen McCarthy, and Kate Messner to ask them about their experience writing books for teachers, each of them provided helpful information and encouragement. Later in the process, J. Todd White, Kristine Redlien, Pamela Courtney, and Towanda Harris served as readers and offered valuable feedback before the book was published. And John Schu revealed the cover of the book on his blog and on social media.

Speaking of publishing, a number of people on the Stenhouse/Routledge team supported the publication of this book, including Sarah Fish, Samantha Meagher, Melanie Moy, Helen Strain, and Nigel Turner.

This book would not have been possible if I had not had thirty years of experience as an educator in elementary, middle, and high school classrooms. Though most of my classroom work with writing goals was done in the middle school classroom, all of the classroom settings I've been in have influenced my work and the strategies that I've provided. Therefore, I have to give a shout out to the teachers with whom I've taught in Greenwich Public Schools and all of the students I've been blessed to teach.

I started asking my eighth-grade students to set writing goals after the Language Arts Coordinator of my district, Marie Jordan-Whitney, invited Educational Consultant Marc Marin to provide professional development to middle school ELA teachers. Marc shared ideas and strategies to guide students on a path to become better writers. The professional development Marc provided, and the specific goal-setting process he guided us through, laid the groundwork for the work that I did with my own students. Later, I shared what I learned with other teachers in my role as an instructional coach. One of the teachers with whom I collaborated, Julia Fama, was kind enough to share some data from work that we engaged in together with her students.

My own teachers encouraged me as a writer. It started in elementary school, when I showed my first early "poems" – rhyming nonsense, really – to Mrs. Toth, my first-grade teacher, and when my sixth-grade teacher, Mrs. Allen, used these words to describe my writing, "Valerie has exceptional flair in this area."

I know from personal experience the difference teachers make in the lives of children and their impact on inspiring children to learn and thrive in their classrooms. So, I want to give kudos to everyone who has a role in helping children achieve their goals and dreams.

1 Why Goal Setting Matters

MY STORY

Writing this book was a lesson in goal setting. I've written poems, articles, and books for children, but, before this, I'd never written a book for teachers. This was a completely new experience for me, and though I'd been an educator for thirty years, I still wondered if I was the person to write this book. In particular, I doubted if I'd have enough to say about the subject, especially when I was told that I'd need to write a minimum of 30,000 words. That number alone was almost enough to make me say "No way!" immediately. Since the shortest book I've written is thirty words, and my longest is about 700, the thought of writing a 30,000-word book was daunting.

While I was deciding whether or not I would pursue this writing endeavor, I remembered that an upcoming week-long writing retreat was on my calendar. I needed a project to dive into during that time, and this book project seemed like the right one. If I wanted to spend time writing during my retreat, that also meant that I would need to work on a proposal and outline prior to leaving. Since I knew the date of my retreat, I worked backward to figure out when I'd need the proposal and outline done, so I could get feedback from my editor beforehand. We had a conversation before my retreat, and I also set up time to speak to her while I was away. I knew that this would be important not only to keep me on track, but also to check in to see if what I was writing met her expectations. Thus, I scheduled three meetings with her during my retreat, and I'm so glad I did because those meetings contributed to my ability to write this book.

Fortunately, because I know myself well and how I work best, I knew that the only way I would be able to complete this writing task would be to set goals. Setting goals motivates me, helps me accomplish what I need to do, and brings me satisfaction. It's like making a list of items and checking them off. I'm the kind of person who enjoys that, and I generally have success completing items on my lists. That's the great thing about goal setting. It works well for those who like to get things done in a designated amount of time, and it also works well for those who need more motivation.

I'm accustomed to setting goals because I've set goals throughout my life, personally and professionally. Each year my husband, Sheldon, and I set goals as individuals and as a couple. For instance, I've created personal goals about exercise, healthy eating, and planning special jaunts with Sheldon. As a couple,

Sheldon and I have created goals centered around donating to a scholarship fund, planning particular vacations, and reading books together. I've also created goals related to my career as an author.

Even my path to becoming a children's book author started with a goal I set in 2017 to explore the possibility of writing children's books. I reached out to those I thought would have helpful information to share; I created an online folder of resources; I went to libraries and bookstores to do "research" (reading children's books and taking notes); I wrote stories, and I took a writing class for children's book writers.

As an educator for thirty years, I created goals for myself related to what I wanted to learn or do better. One year, as an eighth-grade teacher, I wanted to learn more about making the curriculum more engaging for my students, so I attended workshops about dramatizing content and making classical literature relevant. This was a goal I enjoyed working on and accomplished—just like my author goal—but I haven't achieved every goal I've set. Even for those I haven't, I've learned lessons along the way about what leads to success.

So you might be wondering what my own goals as a writer, teacher, and individual have to do with the topic of this book, helping *students* set and work toward goals. The ability to set goals and work strategically toward them isn't a skill we're necessarily born with. It's one we learn along the way in life, through successes and failures, and—if we're lucky—with the help of those more experienced to guide us.

In this book, I'll share glimpses into my process for goal setting as a writer and ask you to reflect on goal setting in your life. And, perhaps most importantly, we'll consider how these experiences might shape the way we teach students to set goals. In particular, I've witnessed how goal setting with students can lead to significant gains. These gains are not only higher test scores and grades, but gains that I might argue are even more important: confidence, perseverance, and self-reflection.

WHY I WROTE THIS BOOK

Goal setting is a natural part of life. We all have things we'd like to achieve, ideas and hopes we'd like to bring to fruition. Many of us start each new year by making New Year's resolutions, which are essentially goals that we want to achieve by the end of the year. Athletes set goals for improving their performance; CEOs set goals for their companies to increase sales and productivity; teachers set goals at the beginning of a school year—professional goals for their own growth as well as student outcome goals for the growth of their students.

I wanted to write this book to show you how to guide your students through setting goals to build agency, independence, and success. Chase Nordengren, in his book *Step Into Student Goal Setting: A Path to Growth, Motivation and Agency*, writes that:

> *Completing a goal—any goal—requires persistence. When learning to cook, few people come right out of the gate making delicious, mistake-free meals. Instead, becoming better at cooking means enduring a lot of cut fingers and inedible meals in the process of becoming the chef you want to be. To make an omelet, you have to break some eggs—and to learn to make a delicious omelet, prepare to break a hundred more (2022, 19).*

Yes, setting and achieving goals in school is worthwhile in itself, but even more important are the life skills students will learn through the goal-setting process.

Oftentimes in school, teachers, and other adults, tell students what they must do and even how to do it. But think about how much more meaningful and empowering it is to have students select the goals they want to work on and to make a plan for how they will go about achieving them. Throughout this book, I'll share my personal experience to demonstrate this concept.

As a teacher, I have witnessed the difference between self-selected goals and school-selected goals. There have been years when my colleagues and I were told what goals we had to choose. These goals may have been a fit for some, but certainly not for everyone. Then, there were years where we were able to determine what goals we wanted to choose and what resources and professional development would be helpful to us in achieving our goals. My colleagues and I were much more invested in our goals during those years when we were able to self-select our goals, and we often made greater progress. Even more significant was that if you asked us what our goals were during the years in which we selected our own goals, we were able to name them, but in the years where we were told what goals we had to choose for ourselves and our students, we often couldn't remember them, unless we looked at the document on which we'd written them.

Our own experiences having and not having agency over our goals can help us understand why it is so critical that students, themselves, learn to set goals that are meaningful and relevant to what they want to achieve.

Educator Regie Routman emphasizes the importance of helping students choose goals that are significant to *them*, not just to teachers, the standards, or the curriculum. "Goal setting for and with students is crucial but only if the goals we set are meaningful and lead to increased student learning, engagement, and even enjoyment ... Ultimately, of course, we want students to be able to set their own worthy goals" (Ferlazzo 2017). Just as with adults, the work of goal setting with students will be infinitely more enjoyable and successful if we focus on goals that students have selected and care about.

One of the benefits of focusing on students being the ones who choose their own goals, and decide how to work toward them, is that it offers us, as teachers, a chance to step back and consider the kind of writers our students want to be and the kind of writing they want to do. Since we're working within the confines of "school writing," we must recognize that this inherently privileges some kinds of writing and voices over others. Therefore, it's important to be aware of our biases and not let them interfere with the agency students should have in setting their own goals. At its best, the goal-setting process opens up opportunities for students' diverse identities to shine in the goals they choose and to decide when they've reached a goal or are ready for a new one.

Nevertheless, even meaningful, self-selected goals are sometimes forgotten. Sometimes goals are too lofty and unattainable. Sometimes they aren't accompanied by a clear plan—specific strategies and a timeline for achieving them. And, often, they go unmonitored because there's no accountability. In this book, however, I'll share with you how to create a classroom environment in which setting goals and reflecting upon their progress is part of the normal routine. You'll guide students through setting realistic, attainable goals with specific strategies for achieving them. You'll teach students how to plan for checking in on and assessing progress toward goals, too. I'll be honest. This goal-setting work will require targeted lessons—which means time—to put these routines and processes in place, but once students know the expectations, they themselves will be primarily in charge of monitoring their own progress. While these lessons may take some "extra" time as you get started, the goal is that they become integrated into your normal lesson plans and classroom routines.

If you want to create a classroom environment where everyone learns together, shares with each other, and encourages and celebrates each other's achievements, then adding goal setting to your repertoire is a smart instructional move. In addition to helping students set goals, monitor progress, and celebrate their achievements, you will set your own goals, too, so you are learning alongside your students and serving as a model for them.

WHY I CHOSE TO FOCUS ON GOAL SETTING IN WRITING

You and your students can set goals in many aspects of your life, and I hope you will. However, the work of this book focuses on writing. As a writer and a teacher of writing, I have a personal connection to establishing writing goals for myself and with my students. In fact, building a community of confident, competent writers was what I most strived to do as a classroom teacher.

The strides that my students made while working on their writing goals were outstanding. In many cases, they surpassed their own expectations. Students who entered the year proclaiming, "I don't like writing" or "I can't write," ended the year feeling confident about their writing and even admitted to enjoying it. Moreover, though test scores are not the only measure of success, my students' writing scores on state standardized tests improved substantially. During one school year, students in my on-level English class made an average growth of 45 points on state assessments from grade seven to eight. The least amount of growth made by a student was 23 points, and the greatest amount was 111 points. The numbers were even higher for students in my advanced classes with an average growth of 72 points, and the largest growth for one student was 152 points. Perhaps what was most fulfilling and exciting, however, is that my students won writing awards and had their work published in poetry anthologies and the school literary magazine.

While the gains my students made as writers were worthy of celebration, I hope that what they learned extended beyond writing. After all, working on writing goals is good practice for any kind of goal where it's necessary to work hard to see improvement.

I was also fortunate to share the practice of setting goals in writing outside of my eighth-grade classroom. As an instructional coach, I worked with middle and high school teachers across my school district in all subject areas. I worked with a middle school English Language Arts teacher for several years, and our work included a focus on goal setting. She said this about our collaboration:

> *Working with the concept of goal setting can be intimidating for both the teacher and the student. However, my work with Valerie transformed my teaching practice to allow for daily opportunities for my students to identify weaknesses in their writing, set goals for improvement, and reflect on their progress.*

In addition to this teacher recognizing the value of students setting goals, her students also echoed this same sentiment. As we looked at comments from her students about how they grew as writers as a result of goal setting, one student wrote on her daily goal-setting sheet:

> *Today, I focused on stretching a moment in my piece using dialogue. My goal was to read over my draft and see where I could stretch a moment in my piece using dialogue to show my reader my character's emotions. I was able to do it and added more dialogue. Tomorrow, I will revise my writing by stretching a moment in my story that doesn't include dialogue.*

Grades and surveys in this teacher's class also indicated work on goal setting paid off. On a literary response assignment, the teacher reported that her students improved by 25 percentage points after implementing goal setting as part of her writing instruction. A survey conducted at the end of the year showed that 95% of her students felt confident in their ability to set goals for themselves.

The impacts of goal setting in writing can be observed in a myriad of big and small ways. From improvement in grades on tests and written assignments, to teachers' observations of students' progress as writers, to (and this one is the most important) students taking responsibility for and reflecting upon their own learning, it is clear that investing time and effort in teaching students to set goals yields positive results.

HOW THIS BOOK WORKS

Students—like all of us—have to do a lot of writing to get better at writing. They need frequent and varied opportunities to practice writing if they're going to work on writing goals. Therefore, before we take a look at how the book works, I want to be transparent about the fact that this book presumes that writing is a focus in your classroom. If students write only once or twice a week and/or are assigned only one longer piece of writing to do per month or per unit, that's just not enough. Goal setting works best when we are continuously chipping away at our goals, rather than just revisiting them only once in a while. Giving students ample opportunities to write, along with specific writing instruction and feedback, ensures that they have the chance to work toward their goals bit by bit.

Now let's turn to take a look at the structure of this book, so you'll know how it works and what you can expect. In each chapter, I'll start with a story from my own experience to set the stage for and provide insight into what you will learn in the chapter. We'll explore together why a certain aspect of goal setting is important and how you might teach this concept to your students. In each chapter, I'll share a sample lesson, provide questions for you to reflect upon, and invite you to set a goal for yourself. Throughout most chapters, I offer organizers and charts you can use or adapt to support students throughout the goal-setting process. Full-sized versions of these organizers and charts can be found in the appendices and in the support materials online. In particular, I share a visual of the entire goal-setting process in Appendix N that you might share with students as they engage in this work.

MORE ABOUT THE SAMPLE LESSONS

Since everyone writes lesson plans differently, I decided to create a sample lesson model that, hopefully, can be adapted to whatever format you're currently using. Below is the model I'll use and a description of what you can expect in each section.

Please note that some lessons may take more than one session, depending upon the grade level and readiness of your students, as well as the amount of time your teaching schedule allows for writing. And, of course, feel free to adapt parts of my lesson, or create your own entirely. As we know, there can be much variability from classroom to classroom, teacher to teacher, and student to student. One of the things to keep in mind is that even if your students are older or able to work at an advanced level, they will likely be novice goal-setters. Not many students are expert goal-setters because it's not a common practice in most classrooms.

SAMPLE LESSON STRUCTURE

Note: The suggested number of minutes for each part of the lessons may vary slightly from classroom to classroom. The intent, however, is that you prioritize the "Do It" time so that most of the lesson time is spent with students doing the work of the lesson.

Model Each lesson starts with an example that can be shared with your students. While sharing this model, you will also state the goal of the lesson/what you want students to learn. (10–12 minutes)

Respond It's important to provide time for students to think about and respond to the model and to what they're being taught. You may call on a few students to share their thoughts and observations with the whole class, or you may ask them to turn and talk with a classmate sitting nearby or share in a small group. (3–5 minutes)

Try It Instead of asking students to jump into the lesson/assignment right away, I recommend that you give them a bit of time to practice first. This practice should be quick, but it's worthwhile. Sometimes students dive into an assignment and get stuck because they didn't have the opportunity to practice first. Sometimes students begin working and are not following instructions. Other students aren't sure how to begin at all. This "Try It" time allows students to identify both what they do understand and where they're having difficulty. Then, as you circulate around the classroom, you can see where trouble might be bubbling up and where to provide support. When you do ask students to continue the task on their own, the observations you've made during this "Try It" will allow you to know who may need a bit more assistance and who you may even want to pull into a small group or work with one-on-one. (5–7 minutes)

Questions We always want to provide time for students to ask questions as they get started on an assignment. Invite students to check in with a partner first—before asking you—about what they understand and what questions they still have. Sometimes asking a classmate first clears up a student's question, and they no longer need to ask you. That way, when you do ask the group if anyone has questions, you can say something like: "What questions do you have about what we'll be working on today? It may be a question you or someone else had." (1–2 minutes)

Do It This is the part of the lesson where students will continue working on the task. You will make the expectations clear for what should be accomplished during class time. It's possible students will even set goals for what they plan to accomplish during this time. You should also use this time to meet with small groups of students and/or confer with students one-on-one. (While the majority of the lesson time will be spent here, be sure to save time for the "Share" and "Reflect.") (20–30 minutes)

Share I believe it's important to leave time at the end of a lesson to share. Even if students haven't finished an assignment, it's still beneficial to leave at least a few minutes at the end for sharing. It gives students an opportunity to gather new ideas from classmates, celebrate a success during the lesson, and gain motivation to continue the work. This sharing time can be done whole class, with a small group of students, or with a partner. As you're observing and meeting with students, be on the lookout for students who have work worthy of sharing. You can ask these students if they would be willing to share with the whole class, or you can open it up to volunteers. (1–2 minutes)

Reflect Since reflection is such an important part of the goal-setting process, make an effort to reserve time for individual reflection at the end of the lesson. I realize, however, that there may not be time for both sharing and reflection in every lesson. If there isn't time for both, you may, at times, choose to substitute the reflection for the sharing. (2–3 minutes)

Again, these are the components of a lesson plan that I believe are important. There are certainly others you could include, and not everything in this format may work for you or your students or for the amount of time you have scheduled for instruction. I trust you to make the suggestions in this book work for you and your students or to come up with your own lesson structure. After all, in each chapter, I'm just providing one sample lesson, so you'll have ample opportunity to create lessons of your own to support this work. My hope is that others in your school, and at your grade level, are doing the same work, so you can collaborate to plan lessons. How wonderful to be part of a school community where both faculty and students are working on goal setting!

REFLECT AND SET YOUR OWN GOALS

Now comes the time when I'm going to invite you to do some reflection of your own. I will ask you to do this in each chapter. Here are some questions to think about now.

- When have you set goals in different areas of your life?
- When have you achieved a goal, and when have you not?
- What has contributed to your goal-setting success, or what *would have* helped you reach your goal?

I'd like for you to set a goal for how you will use this book. Will you plan to read it cover to cover or skim the chapter titles to see what makes sense for you and your students? Maybe you will just look at the sample lessons in each chapter. Do whatever works best for you.

Examples:

1. I will find time in my schedule to read a chapter of this book each week and take notes.
2. I will read one chapter each week and implement what I've learned with students.
3. I will set a goal for what I hope my students will learn or do better this year, and I will read this book with that goal in mind.

I hope you'll find the information in this book useful for yourself and for your students. Though this book primarily focuses on student writing goals, I hope you'll find ways to encourage students to set goals in other aspects of their academic and personal lives. Most importantly, I hope your students will be inspired to take ownership of their learning and become more independent as you guide them through a process of setting and achieving goals.

2 Ready, Set, Goal!

Introducing Your Students to Goal Setting

MY STORY

When I first started writing children's books, I wrote short, rhyming texts about fun topics, like dance, music, swimming, and outdoor activities. Writing these books came naturally to me, probably because, as a first grader, I enjoyed writing rhyming sentences with whatever phonics pattern I'd recently learned in school. For example, when my teacher taught us about words ending in "at," that day after school, I wrote sentences in my black marble composition book, like: "I see a cat. There is a rat. A dog is on the mat." Many years later, I harnessed that love for rhyme to write my books for young readers, like *Let's Dance!*, *Together We Swim*, and *Bing, Bop, Bam: Time to Jam!*

While I enjoy writing rhyming books, I also wanted to explore other genres. Thus, I set goals for writing different types of books. First, I wanted to write an early reader series. The idea of writing books for our youngest independent readers appealed to me because it seemed to be a wonderful way to promote literacy. And I specifically wanted to write for Scholastic because I had attended a presentation given by the Editorial Director of their Acorn early reader series. After that session, I contacted her to ask questions, and she suggested that I read a number of Acorn books, which I did. Eventually, I began to work on my own story—creating a main character, planning out ideas for the series, and beginning to draft my first early reader—using those Acorn books as mentor texts.

I didn't just set a goal of writing an early reader series; I worked toward my goal by researching the series and planning out what I'd write. Additionally, I set a goal to write my story—and proposals for the next stories in the series—by a certain date because Scholastic had put out a call for stories featuring BIPOC characters written by BIPOC creators, so there was a three-month window in which to get this all done. I guess my strategies worked because when my agent submitted the manuscript and proposals for subsequent books to Scholastic, they offered to acquire the series.

Similarly, when I decided I wanted to write a picture book biography, I read a plethora of picture book biographies. Since I knew I wanted to write about a Black woman, I made sure to seek out and read biographies about BIPOC people. I reached out to author-friends who had written picture book biographies to ask about their process. I also attended several webinars about writing nonfiction picture books, including biographies, and I enrolled in a mentored critique group with an editor who is known to be an expert in children's nonfiction, including picture book biographies. The feedback she provided on my manuscript during the course was invaluable, and when my agent sent the story to publishers that he hoped would be interested in acquiring it, that editor is the one who made an offer.

What do you notice about how I set goals as a writer? Is it similar or different to how you set goals in your own personal or professional life? You might notice, in reflecting on your own goals, or in reading about mine, that I selected goals that were of interest to me. If someone had told me, "Valerie, you should write a novel for adults," I probably wouldn't have gotten very far with that goal because writing a novel isn't a goal I would choose for myself, and it isn't meaningful to me. It's not difficult to understand that the same is true for our students. "Meaningful goals," writes Chase Nordengren, "are a concrete clue to a learner's identity: They highlight why the learner wants to learn and connect the lesson of the day or the week to an overall set of knowledge and skills that will help the learner build a meaningful life" (2022, 20).

Perhaps the most rewarding part about teaching goal setting in the classroom is that the lessons students learn go beyond the school walls and beyond the school year. You can teach students how setting goals will help them not only in your class but also in other parts of their lives. For instance, when I taught my students how to become better writers, I considered it a gift I was giving them for life. Teaching students how to set goals is a similar gift. Just as we use writing in many aspects of our lives, we can set goals in different parts of our lives.

Choosing meaningful goals may be a first step in goal setting, but it isn't the only step. In this chapter, we will take a look at a process for setting goals and consider how to get started teaching students about this process.

WHY SETTING GOALS MATTERS

Most of us want to be the best we can be and do the best we can do. This is true for students as well. Often students and the schools they're in are measured not only by their progress but, ultimately, by their grades and test scores. But like you, I know that grades and test scores are only part of the picture. They can only tell us so much. Beyond test scores and grades, we want students to be confident learners. And more important than having a grade determine their success, we want them to recognize their own success and to know that it's a direct result of choices they've made and positive actions they've taken. We also want students to build habits that will help them outside of school and throughout their lives. When we have students create their own self-selected goals, it doesn't just lead to academic success, it also grants students agency over their own learning. Selecting and setting goals helps students figure out what they do best as learners; it helps them figure out what they should continue to do and where they may need support to continue to grow. Overall, setting goals is a smart instructional move.

A PROCESS FOR SETTING GOALS

So, what are the takeaways from my experiences as an author that can be applied to students who are setting goals?

1. First of all, I chose the goals I wanted to work on. I looked at my currently published books and decided what I wanted to write and publish next. When I realized all of my books were rhyming, I knew that I also wanted to write books that didn't rhyme. When I noticed that all of my books were fiction, I decided to try to write a nonfiction book. I made thoughtful choices about how I wanted to progress in my career as an author.

   Similarly, students must be given the opportunity to choose their own goals. This can be tricky in school. It's convenient for teachers just to tell students what their goals should be. We often have an idea of what students should learn next, and there's the added pressure of ensuring that students meet certain standards and learning targets. But setting goals *for* students doesn't prepare them for setting goals in their lives beyond school. Yes, students' first goals may be a bit clunky, and they will often require revision. What's most important, however, is they will have agency over their goals and learn the skill of choosing what matters to them and setting a course for getting there. So, with this in mind, the first step students should take is to look at samples of their current work—short answer responses, longer pieces of writing, and assessments—and decide where they'd like to go next. Would they like to try to learn something new, or do they want to improve a particular skill? Of course, they can make this decision with your guidance and consultation, but, ultimately, it should be the students self-selecting their goals, not you.

2. My goals, as an author, were specific. I didn't just say, "I want to write something besides short, rhyming picture books." I clearly named what I wanted to write. For example, I didn't just set out to write an early reader series; I aimed to write one for Scholastic Acorn. And when I decided to write nonfiction, I was specific about the type of book: a picture book biography about a Black woman children (and adults!) should know about.

   Students, too, must create specific goals. Often, students may say, "I will do better in math," or "I will get a better grade in science," or "I will become a better basketball player." When students (and adults!) create goals that are too broad, it can be hard to plot a course to achieving those goals and monitor progress along the way. Perhaps these goals might be revised in these ways: "I will do better on the next math test," or "I will improve my lab reports," or "I will work on scoring more rebounds."

   Indeed, one interesting study of goal setting in a fifth-grade language arts class found that setting specific and relevant goals is, at first, challenging for many students. "Students who have learned to follow adult expectations are often at a loss when first asked to set standards for themselves or identify what they want to learn" (Carroll and Christenson 1995, 44–5). Nevertheless, the teacher and researcher in this study found—as you may find with your own students—that when students were engaged in instruction and discussion around goal setting, they learned to set and work toward more specific and meaningful goals (Carroll and Christenson 1995).

3. What truly gives us the best chance of achieving our goals are the strategies we implement. I won't say that goals without strategies are destined to fail, but I will say that they're not given their best opportunity to succeed. That brings me to the third point I want you to notice about the goals I set for the new types of stories I wanted to write. I didn't just name specific goals; I put strategies in place to be successful. Some of these strategies were resources, like the people I reached out to ask for guidance and advice. Others required more work from me, like reading Scholastic Acorn books and picture book biographies. Attending webinars to learn more about nonfiction, researching the subject of my biography, and planning characters and plots for my early reader books were also strategies I put in place to achieve my goals.

Just as with setting goals, developing strategies for meeting those goals is something with which many students lack experience. But with practice and coaching from a teacher and peers, they will grow in these critical skills.

So, let's talk about how you can do this goal-setting work with your students. Throughout this book, I'll share how I have guided my students through the process of setting their goals, and, hopefully, you'll find ideas that work for your students, too. I'll mainly talk about setting writing goals because I did this work with my eighth-grade English students; however, students of any age can set goals in any subject and can even set goals related to behavior and study skills. In other words, the key components I share can be transferred to other areas.

A good first step to begin this work is to have a general discussion with your students about goals before diving into setting academic goals. That way students will recognize that goal setting is already a part of their lives, and asking them to transfer that experience to the school setting should make sense to them.

FIVE "ASKS" TO GET STUDENTS STARTED WITH GOAL SETTING

1. Ask students how many of them play sports or an instrument. For those who do, you can ask if they've ever set goals to improve their performance or if a coach or music teacher has set goals for them. For those who haven't set goals, you can ask if they've ever made New Year's resolutions or if they know someone who has done so. If you happen to have any students who haven't made resolutions or set goals, you can tell them that they're going to have the opportunity to do so in your class.
2. After polling students on their past goal-setting experiences (Step 1), invite them to share one of these goals. I like to have students share first with a partner or in smaller groups, and then I invite them to share aloud either one of their own goals or (with their partner's permission) a goal they heard someone share. After sharing these goals or resolutions, you may ask students to share which goals they've achieved and how they did so. You may also ask which goals they haven't achieved and why they think that they didn't. Anything that gets them reflecting upon goals and talking about them is good. The more students can name what worked well and what didn't, the better. At different points in this discussion

(such as before sharing with classmates), you might require students to jot notes in a notebook or in a digital document. You'll want them to retain this thinking and be able to refer to it as they continue to work through this process.

3. Ask students what actions they took to help them achieve their goals. You may notice that some students may not have much to share at this moment. They may have set goals, but they may not have necessarily come up with a plan for how to achieve their goals. This is a perfect time to talk about strategies. Students need to know that it is difficult to achieve goals without having specific ways to get there. For instance, let's go back to the goals I set as an author. One strategy I implemented was to read many books in the genre I wanted to write, and another strategy was to learn from others. (By the way, you may share with your students the examples from my author goals, or you may share examples from your own goal-setting experience.)
4. Ask students to brainstorm strategies that would have helped them achieve their goals. They may work on this as individuals, or students may work in groups of three and four. They can choose one group member's goal and, together, brainstorm strategies that could work for that goal. Then you can facilitate a whole-class discussion about the strategies. You might ask students to think about if achieving goals might be more successful, using these specific strategies, and why or why not.
5. Ask students if they have any questions. You'll want to allow time for students to process what they learned about setting goals by writing down some thoughts they can share with you. You might ask them to write something new that they learned and a question they have. If they don't have a question—there are always students who say they don't have questions—then you can ask them to share what they will remember or what they would tell someone about what they learned.

All of this may be enough about goal setting for one day, but if you have more time, or skipped some of the steps above, you might be ready to move into actually guiding students to create their own goals. One of the things I like to do to segue into that work is to ask students to think about how many of the goals we discussed were academic goals. This is always interesting because there are usually some goals that are related to academics, but many of the goals students choose to talk about are not, which provides the perfect opportunity to make the point again that we can set goals in all areas of our lives. It's now time, though, to tell students that they will move on to creating academic goals. As I said earlier, the majority of the work I did around goal setting was related to writing, so that's what my examples will focus on. However, you can encourage students to set goals in other subjects and other parts of their lives as well.

TEACH STUDENTS TO SET SPECIFIC GOALS

When I tell students that we're going to create writing goals, I explain to them why. Admittedly, I'm biased as an English teacher and author, but I explain that writing is an invaluable skill that will be used throughout our personal, academic, and professional lives.

You don't want students making up writing goals out of thin air. You want them to create goals worthy of achieving—indicative of what they really want to learn, improve, or accomplish. And you want them to ground their goals in actual data. That's why it's a smart idea to plan the first writing goal lesson after students have written a few papers—usually a couple of short assignments and maybe a longer one—because you'll want them to look at the feedback you've given them to help inform their goals. If they have it readily available, you can also invite them to look at their writing from other classes or from the previous year. Additionally, if the information is available, and your school has a protocol for discussing this information with students, you could also have them look at their most recent standardized test scores in writing. All of this information can be used for students to analyze and figure out what they need to work on as writers. There may be many goals that they could work on, but that's why they get to choose. After all, no one can work on everything at once, and if a goal is achieved, another can be added.

In the past, I've encouraged students to create three goals—two goals related to the quality or content of their writing, and one goal about the mechanics of writing. I have come to realize, however, that some students are better off creating just two goals, and I've even had ambitious students who wanted to create four goals. Therefore, adjust the number and type of goals based on your students. You may even have students who you want to start off with just one goal, and when that goal is achieved—or significant progress is made—you can ask them to add another goal at that time.

You may want students to list goals directly in their notebooks or in a digital document. You may even choose to give students an organizer on which to write their goals. Feel free to create your own organizer or chart for students, or use the example organizers shown in Figures 2.1 (Appendix A) and 2.2 (Appendix B).

As students are working on their goals, you'll want to circulate around the room and check in with them.

Goal Setting Organizer

Name: ______________________________ Date: ____________

Choose **THREE** goals to work on in all of your written assignments. Write them down in simple statements. Please select **TWO** goals for writing (content/quality) and **ONE** goal for editing.

After you have chosen your goals, select strategies you will use to achieve them. You must write at least **TWO** strategies for each goal.

MY WRITING GOAL	STRATEGIES/HOW I WILL WORK TOWARD MY GOAL
Example: I will work on organizing my thoughts and ideas in my writing.	1. I will carefully plan my writing before I begin to write. 2. I will work on my transitions from one thought/idea to the next so that my writing flows in a logical way.

FIGURE 2.1 Goal Setting Organizer

Goal Setting Organizer with Check-in Dates

Name: ______________________________ Date: ___________

Choose **THREE** goals to work on in all of your written assignments. Write them down in simple statements. Please select **TWO** goals for writing (content/quality) and **ONE** goal for editing.

After you have chosen your goals, select strategies you will use to achieve them. You must write at least **TWO** strategies for each goal.

Date of First Check-in Toward Progress:
Date of Second Check-in Toward Progress:
Date of Third Check-in Toward Progress:
Date of Final Check-in Toward Progress:

MY WRITING GOALS	STRATEGIES/HOW I WILL WORK TOWARD MY GOAL
Example: I will work on organizing my thoughts and ideas in my writing.	1. I will carefully plan my writing before I begin to write. 2. I will work on my transitions from one thought/idea to the next so that my writing flows in a logical way.

FIGURE 2.2 Goal Setting Organizer with Check-in Dates

Once the goals are set, then it's time for strategies. Recall that when I wanted to learn more about different genres and, ultimately, write books in those genres, I didn't simply say I wanted to accomplish those goals. I developed a clear plan with strategies for how I was going to achieve my goals, like reading many books in those genres and speaking to other authors who were writing those types of books. This is a good time in the goal-setting process to have students work with a partner or in small groups to share their goals and to brainstorm strategies. Eventually, all of the goals and strategies can be shared on a class chart or digital document, such as the one in Figure 2.3. You don't need to

SUGGESTIONS FOR GOAL-SETTING STRATEGIES		
TYPE OF GOAL	**IF THIS IS YOUR GOAL...**	**HERE ARE SOME POSSIBLE STRATEGIES YOU MIGHT TRY...**
Creating Captivating Beginnings	I will work on exciting leads/hooks.	• I will refer to my notes on the lessons my teacher taught about writing strong hooks and leads. • I will read a number of different beginnings in books and/or my classmates' writing to get ideas for how to write my own strong beginning. • I will write several different beginnings/leads to see which one works best. • I will ask for feedback on the different leads/hooks I've written. • I will ask myself if my lead is not only engaging but if it also sets up the rest of my story or essay.
Adding Dynamic Details	I will add specific details to my writing.	*For Responses to Literature and Essays* • I will add examples from the text. • I will add direct quotes from the text. • I will add statistics and/or anecdotal data, if appropriate. • I will keep a list of ideas/information as I read that I may be able to use in my writing. • I will make a comparison to another text or piece of information, if appropriate. *For Creative Writing* • I will add dialogue. • I will add internal thinking. • I will show instead of tell. • I will take a moment from my writing and slow down the action, frame-by-frame, to make it more exciting. • I will paint a picture with words, describing a scene or action in detail.
Using Words That WOW	Instead of using boring words or the same words over and over, I will use a variety of words.	• I will look for repeated words and swap them out for other words. • I will use a thesaurus. • I will add similes, metaphors, and other figurative language. • I will use strong verbs. • I will avoid words, like "stuff," "things," and "said."
Using Proper Punctuation	I will work on using commas correctly.	• I will review my notes on the lessons my teacher taught about correct comma usage. • I will read my writing aloud to listen for natural pauses and places where I may have missed commas. • I will ask a classmate to read my writing to check for missing commas. • I will look for places in my writing where Microsoft Word (or Google Docs) has suggested a comma may be necessary. • I will complete comma practice exercises from an online resource.

FIGURE 2.3 An example of a class chart that can be used for brainstorming and sharing possible strategies for different types of writing goals

attach students' names to them; just listing categories or types of goals and the strategies that might work well is a helpful way for students to learn from one another.

Once students have had time to brainstorm with a partner or small group, and have created a class chart of their ideas, they can then add their strategies to their goals. You might ask students to determine which goal they'll work on first, and perhaps they'll even write in their notebook or on a digital document what they will do first to work toward their goal. You can also ask students what they could take from their writing goals to apply to other goals they might set in another class or outside of school. For example, whatever mechanics goal they're working on in English class can also be applied any time they write. Or, if they're working on adding more details to their writing, they can add more details when writing up procedures in a science lab report.

I've noticed that students sometimes think English class is the only time when they need to write well. I've seen writing that students have handed in for other subjects, for example, explaining how they've solved a math problem, and I'm surprised by the lack of detail and the incorrect spelling and grammar. Thus, I want students to apply these writing goals to *all* of their writing. I also realize that some students may need to create goals related to other behaviors, either before or alongside their writing goals. For instance, some students may need to work on writing stamina as a first goal. They may want to create a goal for how many words or sentences they can write within a certain amount of time. A stamina goal can easily be transferred to other areas of a student's life. After all, some students could benefit from increasing their stamina in reading, in practicing a musical instrument, or in running drills for their sports activity. In addition, sometimes goals change depending upon the writing unit. A student who is working on writing captivating dialogue in a personal narrative or memoir may need to adjust that goal when writing nonfiction. Instead of writing dialogue, that student would focus on including quotes from texts or sources and crediting them appropriately.

SAMPLE LESSON: GUIDING STUDENTS TO SET THEIR OWN GOALS

Model Share an example of a specific goal. (I've included an example from my writing life below, but you may choose something from your life or even an unidentified student's goal.) Ask students to point out what's specific about the goal.

Goal: I will write a Scholastic early reader series.

Strategy 1: I will read at least five Scholastic Acorn books to learn more about the characteristics of these books.

Strategy 2: I will learn from others by contacting the Scholastic Acorn editor and speaking to authors who write early readers.

Strategy 3: I will create a main character and plotlines for the series I plan to write.

Invite students to notice that the goal is specific and that there are strategies listed, which will help with achieving the goal. Determining and working on strategies is an integral factor for experiencing success with a goal.

Respond Give students a few minutes to think about a goal. Have them share a draft goal with the whole class or a turn and talk partner. Partners may even give each other advice on making the goal more specific.

Try It Ask students to write the goal down and make it as specific as they can. You should walk around the classroom, checking to see if students are able to complete the task, and coaching students who may need support. Make note of what students are doing well and where they might be having difficulty, so you can share your observations with the whole class. It's encouraging to compliment what students are doing well and to provide guidance in areas where a number of students may be having difficulty. During this time, you might also make decisions about which students may need to be pulled into a small group, so you can help them complete the task.

Questions Ask students if they have any questions. If students don't ask questions in this moment, you might ask if anyone would like to volunteer to have their goal workshopped by the class. Ask the rest of the class to notice what their peer is doing well and to give suggestions for revising the goal or strategies.

Do It Students will continue writing and revising their goals and strategies, using an organizer such as the ones in Figures 2.1 and 2.2 or in their notebooks. You will set up parameters for the number and types of goals students should write.

Share Save time for students to share their goals with a partner. Perhaps a few students will volunteer to share with the whole class. You or the students sharing will decide whether this is a celebration-only share or if positive and corrective feedback may be given on the goals.

Reflect Offer students the opportunity to reflect upon what they learned about goal setting. They can also write down either what their first step will be to accomplish their goals or which goal they'd like to focus on first.

REFLECT AND SET YOUR OWN GOALS

Think about a goal you've set. It might be a goal you're currently working toward or one you've set in the past. It might be a goal from your personal life or teaching life.

- Was your goal specific?
- Did you name strategies that could help you achieve your goal?
- If you haven't set a goal recently, think of a goal you'd like to set. How could you create one that's specific, and what strategies should accompany it? It may be related to your role as a teacher or not.

Now set a goal for how you will help students set goals.

Examples:

1. I will plan a lesson on goal setting and share some of my own goals with students.
2. I will anticipate what goals students might create and curate a list of strategies that may be helpful to them.
3. I will look at my upcoming lessons and determine which ones would provide an opportunity for students to work on and/or reflect upon their goals.

Now that students have set their goals and chosen their strategies, you'll need to give them practice putting their plans into action. That's done by creating assignments during which they can focus on a particular goal and reflect upon how they did. There also needs to be time built into lessons to monitor progress. I mentioned in Chapter 1 that sometimes goals go unforgotten and unmonitored. We want to make sure that this doesn't happen to our students as new goal-setters. If we believe that setting goals is important and that this process will increase student achievement and independence, then we must weave this work into lessons and assignments, making it a regular part of classroom routines and expectations. I'll share ideas for how to do this in the chapters that follow.

3 "How's It Goaling?" Building a Goal-setting Toolbox with Students

MY STORY

Soon after deciding to write this book, I was fortunate to set off on a writing retreat. Seven days away from the distractions and responsibilities of "real life" seemed like an ideal time to get started on this new-to-me genre (and daunting project!). Despite feeling ready to dive into this work, I also felt a sense of doubt creeping in. My mind flooded with questions, like: Would I really be able to write this book? Did I have enough ideas? Were the ideas good enough? Many writers (and goal-setters of all sorts) experience these kinds of feelings at the beginning of a big project. Luckily, I had a few ideas about what I could do to be as productive as possible during the retreat and to stay motivated. I thought about what would help me be successful, and I utilized these tools, even before I left for my writing retreat. For me, tools are any techniques or supports that can assist me in staying on the path to accomplish my goals.

The first thing I did was decide how much I wanted to write while I was at the retreat. Since I knew the book would be seven or eight chapters in length—and I had a week of concentrated time to focus on this endeavor—it seemed reasonable to strive to write a minimum of three chapters, possibly four, during my time away. I wasn't expecting these chapters to be polished, but I did want them to be fleshed out enough, so that I could fill in gaps and revise later. Truthfully, I originally wanted to commit to drafting the entire book in a week, but, after checking in with a few author-friends who write novels, I realized that would be a lofty goal. When I asked them how many words they generally expect to write in a day, they said anywhere from 2,000 to 3,000 words. Therefore, I decided that writing three chapters might be all I'd be able to accomplish that week. After all, even that might be a challenge for me, as this was my first time writing a book like this. I'd have to exercise different writing muscles. Since I'm used to writing picture books and early readers, I decided that any progress I made should be celebrated. Plus, I was on a writing retreat and wanted to take walks and visit with other writers who were retreating as well. Therefore, writing 2,000 to 3,000 words a day, especially if that's what "the pros" do, seemed to be the most I should realistically hope for.

Once I decided that 2,000 to 3,000 words a day was something to aim for, I measured my word count each day. Occasionally while writing, I would check to see how many words I had written, so I knew how many more I needed to write to meet my goal for the day. In addition, sometimes I used the clock to motivate me. I could have set a timer, but it was easy enough for me to keep an eye on the time at the top of my computer. Sometimes I would break the goal into smaller chunks to see how many words I could write in thirty minutes. Being aware of my word count helped me to push myself and continue chugging along. I'd also reward myself with stretch breaks when I got to a certain word count.

Perhaps what was most helpful to me on this journey was meeting with my editor. Though, of course, her feedback and encouragement were extremely helpful throughout the process, I set meetings with her more as an accountability tool. I knew that if I scheduled meetings with my editor while at the retreat, I would need to have writing—actual chapters—to show and discuss with her. I wanted to have at least two meetings with her while on my retreat, but I scheduled three, and we kept all three of them. The first meeting was to discuss my outline before I set off writing, and when I met with her two days later, I was able to share Chapters 1 and 2. When we met the following day, Chapter 3 was ready. It was validating to know that not only was my editor pleased with my progress but also with the content of what I'd written.

As a writer, I find accountability partners to be invaluable. I'm a member of several critique groups, but I also have a writing partner with whom I check in daily about all things writing. So, I checked in with my partner as well during the retreat to let her know where I was in the process of writing this book. Even with my writing for children, I tell my partner what I plan to work on and what I have completed each day, so I'm accustomed to this back-and-forth with her. Sometimes when I finish what I've set out to do, I send my writing to her. At times, I tell her that she doesn't need to read it; I'm just sending it to her as an accountability action for myself. Though my partner didn't read any of my work for this book, being able to tell her what I was working on and what I had accomplished was helpful throughout the process.

As I ended my time at the writing retreat, I felt satisfied with how much writing I'd done. I hadn't finished the entire book, but I had written four chapters! My writing felt incomplete in places, but there were words on the page, which was my goal. There was something to revise. The tools I used while working on this book—setting word count goals, using the clock to motivate me, and checking in with my accountability partners (editor and writing partner)—all helped me meet my goals, even—and particularly when—feelings of uncertainty arose.

Tools are especially helpful during moments when we're most likely to lose momentum—when the project feels so big, and we have so far to go. Those are also the moments when our tools will keep us moving along the path toward achieving our goals. Students, too, can reap the benefits of using tools to help them achieve their goals. What's great is that most of these tools are readily accessible and easy to use. As a teacher, you will help your students explore different tools and provide guidance and structure throughout the exploration process. Most importantly, you'll schedule time in class to experiment with a variety of tools.

WHY GOAL-SETTING TOOLS MATTER

Setting goals is great, but, unfortunately, after the initial excitement wears off, goals often go forgotten. The New Year's resolution is a distant memory by February. We solemnly pledge to work on our goals daily—and even make a plan to do so—only to tuck that plan away when we hit our first tricky obstacle. Too often, goal setting is an exercise but not necessarily something we focus on and take to heart. For goals to work, and for the goal-setter to see progress, we need to interact with goals often. When we use certain tools to help us with this process, it keeps goal setting at the forefront of our minds and makes it more than a one-time only or twice-a-year check-in activity. This is true for both ourselves, as adults, and for our students. In their study of goal setting in a fifth-grade classroom, Carroll and Christenson emphasized the need to create "an environment to support the goal-setting process ... We saw the need for a classroom structure that would give students many opportunities to work toward the goals they had set for themselves" (1995, 45). In other words, we all need a set of tools if we are to stick with our goals and accomplish them.

You may remember that in Chapter 1, I asked you to reflect on times when you've set goals and what has helped those goals be successful (or not). Perhaps there were certain tools you used that helped you achieve them. If you didn't achieve as much as you hoped, perhaps a tool would have helped you. When I use the term "tool," as I said earlier, I mean anything that will help you achieve your goals, any type of support. Think about what has been helpful to you—or would have been helpful to you—and you may want to share those ideas with your students.

Let's explore how you can teach students to use some of the tools that I used when I shared "My Story" at the beginning of this chapter as well as some other tools. The thing about tools, of course, is that different ones work for different people. Therefore, it's a good idea to introduce a number of options and allow students to choose the ones that are best for them. Have them try out each option—and usually more than once—to see what works for them and what may not. Sometimes we assume that something won't work for us, and then we try it and find out that it actually does. Likewise, we may think something will work well for us, and it doesn't work as well as we imagined. That's why I encourage you to provide opportunities for your students to explore a variety of tools multiple times. Also, remember that in addition to exploring a variety of tools, students need to write frequently and experiment with different types of writing. They may discover that they prefer to switch up their tools based on the writing task at hand.

SEVEN TOOLS THAT CAN HELP STUDENTS WITH GOAL SETTING

1. MAKE A TIMELINE

The first thing I did when I thought about the actual task of writing this book was to consider a timeline. I calculated the amount of time that I was going to be at my writing retreat and, before even arriving, figured out what I could reasonably accomplish. And then I counted the number of days I would be there and decided what I could complete each day. When I returned from my retreat, I figured out how much time I would have left to finish my first draft, being cognizant of my deadline for submitting the completed book. Based on that, I was able to map out a timeline that would provide flexibility, but also wouldn't have me completing the assignment on the day it was due. I knew that I wanted to be finished at least a month ahead of time, so I had time to read the manuscript over, make changes, and ask my editor any last-minute questions before sending it off to her.

Even if students aren't yet taking on a project as big as writing a book, they can also benefit from creating timelines to plan their assignments. Busy students often have a number of assignments, projects, and tests occurring in the same week or even on the same day. Using a timeline technique can help them map out a way to get everything done across their classes or on a single project. Perhaps most importantly, timelines help students avoid having to do everything at the last minute, which creates pressure and anxiety, and can prohibit us from doing our best work.

2. JOT ON A CALENDAR

As I wrote this book, I created my own self-imposed deadlines. Each day I wrote down what I wanted to accomplish. Though I didn't actually use a calendar every day while I was at my writing retreat, I did write my daily goals on a piece of paper. However, when working on other projects, I often use my calendar to list the writing I hope to accomplish on a particular day. And I did make sure to write on my calendar what my next steps for book writing would be when I returned home from my writing retreat. I even scheduled two three-hour blocks on my calendar for my first week back at home. I knew that once I returned home, it would be harder to find chunks of time to work solely on this book, so I wanted to block out the time in advance.

We can teach students how to use a calendar to list/track what they want to work on each day—even within certain hours of the day. For example, they may practice piano on a certain day from 4:30 to 5:00 p.m., or they may work on a writing goal by spending fifteen minutes a day for a week reviewing comma rules. If students don't want to use a calendar, they can use a journal, notebook, or even a piece of paper. The main thing is to write, somewhere, what they want to accomplish within a limited timeframe and then commit to getting it done. Using a calendar, or writing down this information elsewhere, is also a great tool for tracking progress because students will have a record of what they accomplished and when they did so.

3. USE A TIMER

Setting a timer can be an effective tool for many kinds of goals beyond writing. For instance, if athletes are working on a goal to run faster, timing how fast they can run a certain distance is a great way to track progress. A timer also works well if students are working on becoming more fluent readers. For example, there's an exercise I've done with students that requires them to re-read the same passage over and over to try to increase their speed with each reading. Eventually, they will move onto new passages, and the hope is that their improved fluency will transfer. So, even when they're reading something for the first time, it will be at a faster rate than when they started tracking their fluency.

A timer also works well for a stamina goal. Some students find it hard to read for thirty minutes straight. A student can set a timer for ten minutes to start and then add five minutes during subsequent reading times. Before you know it, that student is able to read for thirty minutes. This also works well for improving writing stamina. Some students may feel they're done writing after fifteen or twenty minutes when you want them to get used to writing for thirty to forty-five minutes. A timer can be quite motivating in pushing students to write without stopping for longer time periods.

Specifically with writing goals, students can set a timer to work on a particular goal for a certain length of time, uninterrupted. Timers help us exercise our focus muscles. For example, when I'm working on a project, I usually set a goal to accomplish it (or a designated part of it) by a particular time. However, distractions sometimes tempt me. I might check my email or look at social media for a minute. Fortunately, I'm able to come back to the task quickly, but students (and some adults, too!) can get wrapped up in distractions that can take them away from their work. The next thing they know, thirty minutes or more have gone by, and they've done nothing—or very little. Students are still learning about these distraction traps, so teaching them to use focus tools, like timers, is a skill that will benefit them far beyond the walls of your classroom. They can set a timer for thirty minutes (or whatever amount of time), and, during that time, do nothing else but work on an assignment or study for a test. No texting a friend, no playing video games, no getting something to eat. Nothing. The great thing about timers, too, is that when we accomplish our goal, we can give ourselves a small reward. For instance, I like to reward myself with a stretch break. If I've been working for a long period of time, I may reward myself with a snack. Learning to work without distractions is an important skill for students.

4. COUNT OR MEASURE

It's a known fact that counting and measuring can be motivating and keep us on track. Think about people who are trying to eat healthfully. Some count the grams of protein they eat in a day, the number of fruits and veggies they eat in a week, or keep a diary tracking how they feel after eating certain foods. Students can use a similar technique to track their progress. Remember, I shared that I worked on my goal for this book by keeping track of my word count. Students can do this, too. Perhaps an assignment needs to be a certain number of words or pages, or maybe a student is working on a stamina goal to write more words in a class period or on a particular assignment. Counting is a great way to do this. Fortunately, this can easily be done with the word count tool on computers.

If students don't already know how to use it, please show them. Measuring can help as well. Just as distance runners might set a goal of running more and more miles on their long runs as they train for a race, students can also measure their writing in similar ways. Instead of counting words, we can look at the number of paragraphs or pages. When we count and measure, the data gives us a clear indication of how we are progressing toward our goals.

5. BE ACCOUNTABLE TO SOMEONE

An integral part of goal setting is accountability. There are ways we can be accountable to ourselves. For instance, I create weekly lists and break them down further into daily lists. I don't share these lists with anyone, but writing them—and checking off things as I complete them—holds me accountable for accomplishing a lot each week. As an adult, I can manage this myself, but students may benefit from some explicit teaching about making a checklist of things to do, monitoring the checklist, and knowing what to do when they don't get everything done on their checklist. (Carry it forward to the next day!) Though I love my checklists and can manage them on my own, what I also find extremely helpful is having an accountability partner and/or group. I shared with you how I communicate throughout the day with my writing partner. I also shared that I consulted with the editor of this book throughout the process of writing it and how that not only moved my writing along but also kept me accountable to the timeline I created for myself.

In *The Writing Strategies Book*, Jennifer Serravallo writes about the power of naming our goals aloud to a partner in a lesson she calls "Make Promises (You Can Keep)":

> *Talk with your partner about your goals (for the writing period, for the week, and/or for the writing work to take place at home, and so on). Discuss together how you might get that work done. Write the goal, and make the promise ... then check in with your partner soon (2017, 368).*

You can support your students in setting up these accountability partners or groups that will help keep them on track with their goals. Of course, there will be students who prefer to work alone and not with a partner. There may also be others who need more support than a peer accountability partner can provide; they will need your support to implement and monitor tools for goal setting.

But, even for both of these types of students, peer support is still worthwhile, and students should have the opportunity to try it out to see what they gain from it. To set up accountability partners for the greatest success, consider allowing students to choose their own partners, rather than you assigning them. Students may feel more comfortable sharing their goals and work in progress with someone they know well.

Developing trust with an accountability partner is critical. Ideally, the groundwork will have already been laid, as you've been working consistently to create a classroom environment in which everyone feels valued and in which all voices and opinions matter. When this is part of your classroom norms, the work of accountability partners should run smoothly. You may also consider offering opportunities for accountability partners to give you feedback on how the partnerships are going, so you can teach into any challenges that might come up. For example, at the end of class, you could ask students to write a quick note to you in response to the questions: What's going well with your accountability partner? What could be going better with your accountability partner?

It can also be helpful for you to guide students through options for how they might utilize their accountability partners. It's fine (and expected) that accountability partners will have different goals. They just need to come to an agreement about what they each need and what each is willing to do to support the other. For this to work, the arrangement needs to be agreeable to each partner or everyone in the group. Give students ideas for ways they might check in with their partner. For instance, they might do a quick check-in to say something like: "This is a goal I've set, and I've achieved it," or "This is a goal I've set that I haven't achieved yet, but I hope to achieve it by X time. I'll check back in with you when I've achieved it." If the accountability partner hasn't heard from the partner at the designated time, a gentle check-in might be warranted to provide motivation and support. Some students may want to share counting or measuring data with a partner. If it works for the partner or group, at times, they may want to work on a similar goal together and then compare how it went. Anything that works for the students involved and helps them be more accountable to their goals is worth exploring.

You might even make a simple class chart, such as the one in Figure 3.1 (Appendix C), to remind students of the purpose of accountability partnerships, and include some language they might use when meeting with their partner.

ACCOUNTABILITY PARTNERS SUPPORT EACH OTHER'S GOALS

Here are some ways to check in with your partner.

- How's your goal coming along?
- What strategies are you working on right now?
- When do you plan to finish this?
- Is there anything I can help you with?
- When should we check in on this again?

FIGURE 3.1 Accountability Partner Guidelines

6. FOCUS ON GOALS IN ASSIGNMENTS

For certain assignments, I asked my eighth-grade students to identify which goal they were working on. For example, before getting started on writing a personal narrative, a student might write at the top of her assignment, "I will use engaging and precise verbs." Another student might write, "I will use correct punctuation for dialogue," as his reminder to work on this goal as he writes. Simply stating what goal they're working on causes students to focus on that goal. Of course, they also have to do the work of determining which goal would be appropriate to work on in the particular assignment. Mechanics goals work for any assignment, but a goal about including quotes as supporting evidence may not be a fit for every assignment. On the other hand, adding details works for most assignments, but the type of details a student would include for a memoir will be different than those in an essay.

When I graded my students' assignments, I not only graded them on the assignment itself, but also on how well they worked on their goal. For instance, if a student said they were working on adding specific details, I would provide feedback on how well they had done that, and I awarded a couple of extra points if I felt they did a great job working on their goal. Likewise, if a student wrote a goal at the top of the paper, and I didn't see much evidence of it, I would comment on that and take a couple of points off.

Science educator and education professor Stephanie Toro suggests a similar strategy of asking students to jot down short-term daily goals on sticky notes. "At the beginning of the day, students take a few minutes to imagine some task, behavior, or skill they want to focus their intentions on for that specific day. Let the students keep the notes somewhere visible, so they can refer back to the goal throughout the day" (Toro 2021).

The strength of keep-the-goal-visible tools such as these is that students need to review their goals to choose which one they want to work on for the particular assignment, and, hopefully, determine which strategy will help them achieve the goal. Therefore, this approach is grounded in student ownership. Though I selected the assignments for which students would focus on a goal, I didn't tell students which goal to choose. I was also careful not to ask students to focus on a goal in *every* assignment because I think this tool could lose its effectiveness as often happens when any tool is overused. And though I selected the assignments, it's possible that you could set it up so that your students could determine, maybe three assignments a quarter, when they would specifically work on their writing goals. Of course, we want students to work on their goals consistently, but identifying certain assignments and times when they will do so provides a targeted approach to working on goals. Requiring specific times to work on goals keeps them at the forefront of students' minds.

An extension of this tool could be to ask students to write a couple of sentences about what they did to work on their goal in their assignment and to share whether or not they think they did so effectively. Asking them to share a specific example from their piece of writing that shows evidence of the goal "at work" is a prime way for students to reflect on their progress related to that goal and builds their agency.

7. USE GOAL-SETTING TOOLS IN A VARIETY OF SETTINGS

As an English teacher, I focused on writing goals because I wanted my students to become better, more confident writers. However, goal setting is a skill that can help us achieve success in many parts of our lives. I want you, as teachers, to take what you're reading and learning in this book and be able to transfer it to supporting students in other subject areas, if you teach more than one subject. Likewise, I want students to be able to apply goals to other parts of their lives.

Even a writing goal can be applied to writing outside of the English classroom. For example, when students are writing science lab reports, explaining how to solve a math problem, or creating a political cartoon, I want them to use their best writing skills. After all, if students are to become competent writers, that needs to happen across all subject areas and in their lives outside of school.

Beyond focusing on goals related to writing skills, students can also work on a stamina goal and other aspects of their lives. Students can even transfer the techniques mentioned in this chapter to other parts of their lives. For example, thinking back to the discussion of counting and measuring, those same tools can be used anytime students want to track their progress. When students are able to transfer their knowledge from one situation to another, that's often when true growth occurs. That's a sign that what they're learning is "sticking." And when learning sticks, that's when progress will be made with goals and with whatever we want to achieve.

SAMPLE LESSON: SETTING UP ACCOUNTABILITY PARTNERS

Model Share with students an example from your own life of how you've used an accountability partner, or you can share examples from my experience that I've provided in this book. If you're using your own example, make sure you're specific about what the goal was and how you communicated with your partner about it. For instance, you could say, "When I was packing to move to my new home, I set goals for packing a certain number of boxes a day or packing up a particular room in my house. So, one day I told my accountability partner that by lunchtime, I was going to pack all the books on my bookshelves. Another day, I said that I would pack up everything in my office by the end of the day. I named my specific goals out loud to my partner and told her when I would accomplish them."

Respond Since the accountability partner doesn't necessarily need to do more than listen or cheerlead and encourage, it's possible students may wonder how reporting their progress to a peer can be helpful. Therefore, give students a chance to discuss why accountability partners could be helpful as they work on their goals. If students question what the value of this might be, you can tell them that they should give it a try. Not all strategies work for everyone, but we can't know what might be useful to us without giving a new tool an honest effort. As I said earlier in the chapter, it's important that students try out different tools, so they can learn what works best for them.

Try It Ask students to choose one of their goals that they think would be good for checking in with an accountability partner.

Questions Ask students if they have any questions.

Do It Students should choose their accountability partners and come up with a plan for how they will work together. You know your students best, so ask yourself: "Is it fine to have my students choose partners on the spot, or do I want them to list three people that they believe would make good accountability partners for themselves, and then I'll tell them the next day who their partner will be?" The second option is for cases where you believe some students may not have a partner to choose or may not be chosen. It could also be for a situation in which many students want the same partner, and a student will find it difficult to choose one person. If you end up asking students to write names on a piece of paper, then you can skip to the Reflection. Students can then check in with their accountability partners the next day when you tell them who their partners are.

Once students know who their accountability partners are—either in this lesson or the next day—they should decide what goal they'd like to work on first and how their accountability partner can support them.

You will need to set up a structure for the accountability partner meetings. Though these meetings may not happen within this lesson, I want to provide some tips for making sure students get the most out of these partner meetings. For example, you may allow time for students to meet with their partners twice a week for a couple of weeks for quick check-ins, so they get used to meeting regularly. You will likely need to provide guidance for students about what they should talk about when they meet. It's probably worthwhile to model what this process/discussion could look like. You may want to do that with another adult in the classroom, or you may have a student who would be a willing participant. Also, remind students that they can refer to the accountability partner questions (Figure 3.1 and Appendix C) to guide their discussion. (You may also use it to guide the discussion that you'll model.)

Here's a possible meeting structure. Even though I list two meetings, you can repeat or adjust this structure for future meetings.

1 **Meeting 1:** Take turns sharing the goal you're working on and what you plan to accomplish by a specific date. You can encourage students to ask their partner questions about their goal or offer encouragement.

2 **Meeting 2:** Take turns sharing your progress and next steps. Next steps could be continuing to work on the same goal, using the same strategy; working on the same goal, using a different strategy; or working on a different goal. You can let students know that this would be a good time to compliment their partner for achieving their goal or to encourage them and ask what might help them if they haven't achieved their goal yet. It's also important to point out to students that sometimes goals aren't achieved because they may have been unreasonable, or because—as the saying goes—"Sometimes life happens," and the time we thought we'd have to work on our goal becomes unavailable. This is a worthwhile lesson for students to learn. Being flexible and having the ability to pivot is a great life lesson. You may also want to create handouts or organizers, like the one in Figure 3.2 (Appendix D), for students to track their meetings, what they shared, and what their next steps will be.

Accountability Partner Recording Sheet

After listening to your partner, write one to two sentences describing your partner's goal and plan for moving toward it. After writing these sentences, check in with your partner: "Did I write your goal and plan correctly?" Then, your partner will do the same for you.

Partners' names: ______________________________

Today's meeting date: ______________

______________'s goal/plan:

____

____

____

______________'s goal/plan:

____

____

____

Our next meeting will be ______________ (date).

FIGURE 3.2 Accountability Partner Recording Sheet

Share Students can share their thoughts about accountability partners with a partner (not necessarily their accountability partner but whoever may be sitting near them) during an end-of-class reflection time. They can also share what goal they'd like to try out first with their accountability partner. Perhaps a few students will share with the whole class.

Reflect Offer students the opportunity to reflect upon what they learned about accountability partners and how this tool can help them achieve their goals. They might jot this down for themselves in a notebook or write it on an exit slip to share with you.

REFLECT AND SET YOUR OWN GOALS

Think about your students.

- What additional support could some of your students benefit from as goal-setters?
- Who are the students who may benefit from a different goal, strategy, or tool?
- What can you offer to the students who need something different?

Set a goal for how you will provide tools to students or have them create their own.

Examples:

1. I will analyze my own goal setting to see what tools have been helpful to me or what tools would have been helpful to achieving my goals.
2. I will plan a lesson on the usefulness of tools and share some examples.
3. I will create a list of tools that could be helpful to students as they work on their goals and will post this list where students can easily access it.

As you work on your own goals, you may find yourself creating tools, such as charts, graphs, or webs, that are helpful for you. They may be worth sharing with your students as well to help them track their goal-setting progress. Of course, you can also use and share the charts and forms that appear throughout this book. Your students can design their own tools, too. You may even decide to create a "Wall or Hall of Tools" for students to share what's working for them. This could also be done as a "show and tell" type of sharing. Activities like this reinforce the idea that your classroom is a place where working on goals is part of the normal, expected routine.

4 Giving Goalden Peer Feedback

Helping Your Partner's Work Shine

MY STORY

Writing is often a solitary activity, but when we connect with a community of writers throughout the process, the quality of our writing improves significantly. And perhaps of equal importance, when writers connect with one another, the very act of sharing our work, frustrations, and celebrations can be inspiring and motivating. We feel less alone in the work and ready to move forward with our goals.

I'm fortunate to be a member of several writing critique groups, and my critique partners are integral to helping me shape and refine each draft of my stories. They validate what's working well, offer suggestions for how I can better engage the reader, and provide thoughtful ideas and questions about everything from a particular word choice to a plot point that I hadn't considered. Most of all, they are cheerleaders for my work. They celebrate alongside me when I accomplish both bigger goals (publishing a new book!) and smaller ones (drafting a new story idea). Meeting with my critique partners regularly keeps me accountable and inspires me to continue writing and to make my writing better.

While I enjoy having my writing validated, comments like "I love your story" and "I have no changes to suggest" don't do a whole lot to help me grow as a writer. I yearn for critical critique, not just compliments. For me, the most valuable feedback I receive from my critique partners comes when I direct the discussion by naming a particular kind of feedback I'd like. For instance, I might ask my partners to let me know if the pace of my story is moving along and keeping them engaged or if there are any parts where they felt the story dragged. Other times, when I'm focusing on revising a certain section of the story, I'll ask my critique partners for specific feedback on that part. For example, since I know how vital beginnings are for pulling readers into a story, I often create several options for how my story could start and ask my critique partners to weigh in on which one is the strongest and why. Directing my feedback in this way puts me in control of my story and the type of critique that will help me move forward with my goal. I'm always open to other feedback as well, but setting a goal for the feedback I want to receive is not only helpful to me but also to my partners. It can be difficult to focus equally on every aspect of a story, so this allows my partners to provide feedback that will be most meaningful to me.

Requesting specific feedback is an effective strategy for working toward all sorts of goals. Making a specific feedback request to my partners requires me to articulate my goal clearly—a process that is helpful in itself—even before I have actually received any advice from them. If my goal is to create the strongest beginning I can, and one of my strategies is to write several beginnings, then I'll ask my critique partners to weigh in with their feedback on those beginnings. If my goal is to use figurative or lyrical language in a story, my partners will look for evidence of that in my draft to see how I'm progressing with that goal. They might also point out other places in the writing where I could consider making the language more aligned to my goal.

Yes, my critique partners are an essential part of my writing process, and I'd like to think that they'd say the same about me, since I provide feedback on my partners' stories as well. If they don't name, specifically, what they'd like feedback on, I'll ask them if there's a particular part they're wondering about or if they have any questions about their story. A peripheral benefit of sharing work with critique partners, especially in groups larger than two, is that inevitably you will hear feedback given to someone else that can also be applied to your own writing. Sometimes even when you're offering a suggestion about what a writer might consider, you realize that you could apply this very same suggestion to your own writing as well. Thus, feedback provides an opportunity to learn in unexpected ways. You never know what you may hear that could spark an idea in your own writing.

As a writer, I know the value of feedback in my writing process. I have seen my stories transform as a result of the feedback I've received from my critique partners. Critique partners can also serve as accountability partners. I shared in Chapter 3 that I have a writing partner. She is both a critique partner and an accountability partner, and we share our writing with each other. Having accountability partners sets up a natural segue into peer feedback, so if you've already set up those partnerships in your classroom, it'll be easier for your students to slide into peer feedback. Sharing their writing with others—besides you—and getting feedback on it, allows students not only to grow as writers but also as critical and creative thinkers as they reflect upon the feedback they've received and decide if or how they will implement it. (There will be more about implementing feedback in the next chapter.)

WHY PEER FEEDBACK MATTERS FOR STUDENTS

Getting feedback is beneficial to forward movement. Coaches provide feedback to their players. Conductors provide feedback to musicians, and, as I described, writers give feedback to other writers. And, of course, teachers give feedback to students. Teaching students how to give and receive feedback is an important skill. And while it's a skill that clearly makes sense in the writing classroom, the art of receiving feedback is useful in all kinds of classrooms and beyond the school walls. As the teacher, you can't provide feedback on every assignment, or every step of a process, but students can be taught how to give valuable feedback to each other. Not only can students serve as critique partners, but they can also provide feedback on goals.

You may recall that in Chapter 3, one of the tools I suggested was accountability partners. Feedback partnerships take this tool to the next level. Instead of just checking in with an accountability partner to report progress, students can share feedback with each other by looking for evidence of progress toward goals in each other's work and sharing questions and thoughts about how to work on that goal in a different way.

Learning how to give effective feedback is a skill in itself, and one with which many students may not yet have much experience. It's worth teaching students how to do this, though, since giving and receiving feedback are lifelong skills that students can carry with them throughout their school career and life. In the following section, I will share how you can teach your students to become competent providers and receivers of peer feedback. Though I will focus on providing feedback on writing goals, when students are adept at peer feedback, they can ask for and offer this in other parts of their lives, too. They may ask for feedback on their pitching stance in baseball or their singing pitch, or they may offer feedback on a peer's artwork or short film. Learning how to participate meaningfully in the feedback process means students are taking ownership of their goals and how they will work on them—true agency.

TIPS FOR EFFECTIVE PEER FEEDBACK

BEFORE PEERS SHARE FEEDBACK

1. **Create a Classroom Environment Conducive to Feedback**
   Perhaps the most crucial factor for whether peer feedback will be effective is establishing classroom conditions in which students feel comfortable sharing with each other. You may have noticed that in my sample lesson plans, I always provide opportunities for students to share with

partners (or in a small group) and with the whole class. When students are used to these routines, it sets the stage for solid peer feedback. In addition, if students have been working with accountability partners, they already have experience talking about their goals. Of course, just as there are explicit things you can do to manage the classroom, there are rules and guidelines you can implement to create a respectful, positive, inclusive classroom environment that will facilitate peer feedback.

You may need to do some additional work with your students to remind them to honor each other's differences and that, ultimately, writers get to decide what feedback they'll choose to implement. Writers may also need to be shown what it means to listen respectfully to feedback and not react defensively to a comment or suggestion with which they may not agree. Teachers, too, may have to check our biases and impulses to tell a student the "correct" way to make a change, implying that there's only one way. It can create a lasting impact when we model the behavior of monitoring our own biases and provide a space for students to explore and share theirs.

Establishing norms specific to giving and receiving feedback—and reviewing them briefly before each peer feedback session—can go a long way toward creating an environment in which students feel comfortable sharing. In Figure 4.1 (Appendix E) are some sample charts of what norms might look like, but developing norms alongside your class will have the best chance of success.

2. **Offer Peer Feedback Supports**
   In addition to teaching norms and expectations for peer feedback, you'll find that providing students with other supports can help them be successful. For example, you may want to create organizers to help students take notes and reflect on feedback they receive. These organizers may include sentence starters to guide the discussion. Figure 4.2 (Appendix F) shows one example of such an organizer designed to support students in peer feedback meetings.
3. **Explicitly Teach the Feedback Process**
   Start by having students work with a partner; later you can move to small groups, so students can get wider feedback. If students already have accountability partners, those same classmates could also be their feedback partners, or you may offer them the opportunity to choose someone else.

How to Give and Receive Peer Feedback

When giving peer feedback:

- Listen to your partner.
- Ask, "What would you like feedback on today?"
- Give your partner specific feedback.
- Encourage and celebrate your partner's work.

When receiving peer feedback:

- Come ready to share.
- After sharing, say, "I'm ready for your feedback on [name something specific]."
- Listen to the feedback.
- If you don't understand part of the feedback, say, "Can you explain what you mean by [name point of confusion]?"
- Say, "Thank you for your feedback. I am going to try [name a suggestion your partner has given]."

FIGURE 4.1 How to Give and Receive Peer Feedback

Peer Feedback Form

Name: ______________________ Date: __________

(Fill out before peer conversation.)

Today I want feedback on ______________________

____

____

(Fill out during/after conversation.)

An idea from my partner that I'm going to try is ______________________

____

____

FIGURE 4.2 Peer Feedback Form

You may want to select feedback partners for students, rather than having them choose their own. I believe in giving students some opportunities to select the students they'd like to work with, but students also understand that there are times when I will pick their partners or groups.

Perhaps most critically, you'll need to give students examples of *how* to give feedback. You might want to teach them to start by offering praise (what the partner did well working on their goal). Then they can offer a piece of constructive feedback or something to consider (what the student might do next to work on the goal). This method can be referred to as giving a "praise" and a "polish." You'll also need to teach the person receiving feedback how to ask for specific feedback and how to note what's offered. You might use charts like the example in Figure 4.1 to support students' conversations or a feedback form like those in Figures 4.2 or 4.3 (Appendix G).

Students also need to see effective peer feedback in action. There are a number of ways you might go about this. I provide suggestions in the sample lesson in this chapter. We can tell students what to do, but when they see it and have the opportunity to name what went well, what could be improved, and what they learned that they can bring to their own peer feedback sessions, that's when ownership of learning and transfer occurs.

Praise/Polish/Question Peer Feedback Form

Name: ______________________ Date: __________

This feedback is for ____________________ (partner's name).

I am giving feedback on ______________________________

____

(name writing assignment and goal).

Praise ______________________________

____

____

Polish ______________________________

____

____

Question (Optional) ______________________________

____

____

FIGURE 4.3 Praise/Polish/Question Peer Feedback Form

DURING THE PEER FEEDBACK SESSION

STUDENTS GIVING FEEDBACK

1. **Offer Praise.** Remind students to start by offering praise to their partner before suggesting a "polish."
2. **Be Specific.** You've taught students to be specific when creating their goals and choosing specific strategies to help them achieve their goals. Being specific applies to giving feedback as well. Make sure students know that the more specific the feedback they give, the more helpful it is to their partner.
3. **Share Critical Feedback.** You may need to provide instruction for students about how to offer critical feedback. Giving them examples of how they can phrase suggestions is a good idea. You might ask them to use questions instead of simply telling their partner what to do. Sentence starters can be a helpful scaffold, especially the first few times students give one another feedback. For example, you might suggest that students use phrasing such as, "What would happen if...?", "Have you considered...?", or "Are there other words that could be used for what you're describing?" Figure 4.4 (also Appendix H) shows a sample chart of ways to offer critical feedback. You might start a class chart like this by giving your students some language to use, and come back to it later to add new ways your students have found to offer critical feedback. You might also print small versions of your chart for partnerships to take with them (or put in a notebook) to their meeting spots. Sometimes having a physical support to hold onto in those first peer feedback sessions can make students feel a bit more comfortable with the process.

Ways to Give Your Partner Critical Feedback

- What would happen if...?
- Have you considered...?
- Are there other ways you might...?

FIGURE 4.4 Ways to Give Your Partner Critical Feedback

Giving critical feedback to their peers may feel uncomfortable for students at first. If they stick with it though, they will have learned an invaluable skill for navigating all sorts of situations in life. And once they become more comfortable with critical feedback, you may find that students even prefer it to overly general praise. Brookhart writes:

> *When you do give students information that they can use to improve, and they see and understand that they can do it, research suggests that many—and some cases almost all—students will experience feelings of control over their learning that are so positive that they'll* prefer *constructive criticism to head patting and comments like "Good job!" This feeling of control over learning is true self-efficacy. It is the foundation of motivation for learning (2008, 35).*

While Brookhart writes about the experience of teachers giving feedback to students, I have found this sentiment to be true with peer feedback as well.

STUDENTS RECEIVING FEEDBACK

1. **State Your Feedback Goal.** Be clear with students that they should ask for what they want. They should be proud of their goals and what they're working on and "own" that work by asking for feedback on a goal they've chosen.
2. **Listen and Ask Clarifying Questions.** It can be tempting for students (and even adult writers in critique groups!) to defend and justify, rather than really listen to the feedback they are given. Peer feedback works best, at first anyway, if the student receiving feedback just focuses on listening. Make sure your students know, however, that questions are welcome, especially for clarification. It's essential that they understand the feedback they've been given, so that they can consider and possibly implement it. So, if there's something about the peer feedback students don't understand, they should ask!
3. **Take Notes.** Hold students accountable for taking notes while their partner is offering feedback, or immediately after, so that they can remember it and revisit it later. You may want to create a form to facilitate

this process. I know from experience that if I don't write down all of the feedback I receive, I will forget some of it. Sometimes I even say to my partner, "Hold on. I want to write that down before you continue." Students may not implement all of the feedback they receive—I don't either—but they should consider all feedback, and the only way to do that is if they have a record of it. Students may capture their partner's feedback using the Praise/Polish/Question Feedback Peer Feedback Form (Figure 4.3).

AFTER THE PEER FEEDBACK SESSION

Reflection. An integral part of the peer feedback process is allowing time for students to reflect. You may need to provide some questions to help focus students' reflection. You might ask:

- How did it feel to give and receive feedback?
- What can you work on as a giver and receiver of feedback?
- What feedback did you get that you will use?

While peer feedback should be a part of your goal-setting routine, students should spend time reviewing and revising their work *before* engaging in the peer feedback process. Even I don't share writing with my critique partners that I haven't read over and critiqued myself first. Peer feedback is also not a substitute for teacher feedback. You should continue to check in with students about their goals. As I mentioned in Chapter 3, one way of doing this is to have students identify a goal they're working on at the top of an assignment. Not only does this strategy help students keep their goal in mind as they work, it is also a reminder to you to give feedback on this goal when you review the assignment.

Having conferences with students is also an essential part of the goal-setting process. You can decide when it makes sense to have them and how often. Sometimes teachers do this before the end of a marking period or at a certain point during a unit. While it does take time to meet with all of your students, these feedback conferences provide insight into who your students are and what matters to them beyond their goals. At times, students may also request a conference with you, even if it's outside of the timeframe you've set aside for conferring. Like peer feedback, teacher–student conferences should be led by the student. As Susan Brookhart writes, when you invite a student to lead their conference,

> *it implies the student is someone who thinks, and that the choice the student made had purpose. It invites the student to discuss the choice and presumably go on to discuss whether the paper can accomplish what was intended. It positions the student as the chooser and as someone who can have a conversation with the teacher (2008, 31).*

Therefore, invite your students to lead their conferences. If your students have been participating in peer feedback, then having a conference with you should go more smoothly. If you start with a few peer feedback sessions before students meet with you, they'll be well-practiced and prepared by the time they confer with you.

SAMPLE LESSON: HOW TO GIVE EFFECTIVE PEER FEEDBACK

Model Ask two students if they'd be willing to be recorded or do a live session to demonstrate a peer feedback session. Alternatively, you can record yourself and another teacher having a peer feedback session. Tell students that they will be detectives as they watch the video (or the live session) to note what they see happening. Ask them to notice and respond to the following questions:

- What is Student A doing while Student B is sharing? (Hopefully, listening carefully, looking at their peer, and jotting notes.)
- What is Student B doing when it's time for feedback? (Hopefully, listening carefully, asking for clarification, if needed, and jotting notes.)

Respond Ask students what they notice.

- What type of feedback is being given? Positive? Constructive?
- Is the feedback phrased as statements or questions?
- Did the person receiving feedback determine the focus of the feedback/the type of feedback desired?

- Were any tools used, such as a chart, and, if so, how did the tool help the students?
- What would you do similarly or differently?

Try It Have students practice giving feedback in groups of two. They will need a recent assignment and a goal they're working on. It's best to ask students to prepare for this lesson in advance, so they know which assignment they'll use and what goal they'd like feedback on from their peer partner. To try it out, you may just ask each partner to share the goal they'd like feedback on, and then they can share a few sentences from their assignment, so the peer can provide feedback. Next, the partners can switch roles so that each partner gets a chance to both give and receive feedback.

Questions Ask students if they have any questions and/or how it felt to engage in this activity.

Do It I'm providing two options for this part of the lesson.

1. You may have students continue working with their "Try It" feedback peer or their accountability partner to continue giving and receiving feedback.
2. You may select (with an advance heads-up) one partnership to volunteer to "put their session on display" to continue learning about this process. If you proceed with this option, make sure everyone—those receiving feedback, those giving feedback, and those observing—has a clear task. This activity can be done as a fishbowl activity, with the partnership modeling their feedback session in the center of your classroom, while other students gather in a circle around them to observe. Make sure to debrief what you observed as a class, and thank the partnership who shared for helping the whole class get better at giving and receiving feedback.

Share Give students the opportunity to share. Encourage them to be specific about the experience of giving and receiving feedback. Feel free to use the following questions.

- How did it feel to give or receive feedback?
- What worked well?
- What could be improved?

If you tried Option 2 from the "Do It" section, you may use some of the questions above, but also ask the observers of the peer feedback section what they noticed. You might ask students questions like:

- Did you notice the receiver naming the feedback goal?
- Did you see note taking?
- Did you hear clarification questions?

Reflect Ask students to reflect upon what they will remember to do when giving and receiving feedback. How can they provide better feedback? How can they direct the kind of feedback they want to receive?

REFLECT AND SET YOUR OWN GOALS

Think about how you respond to feedback and how others have responded to yours.

- What have your experiences been with feedback, both giving it and receiving it?
- What lesson(s) will you teach to ensure that peer feedback is given and received appropriately?
- How will you use what you notice about students' reactions to feedback to move learning forward and help students achieve their goals?

Set a goal for how you will plan lessons to guide students through peer revision and how you will assess their effectiveness.

Examples:

1. I will plan a lesson in which I ask students to reflect upon feedback they've received in the past. Some questions I might ask are:
    - What was most helpful?
    - What wasn't helpful?
    - What do you think it means to give good feedback and/or be a good peer feedback partner?

- How can you be better about asking for the feedback you want?
- What goal can you set for yourself to be a better feedback partner?

2. I will create tools, such as sentence starters, to help students provide effective feedback.
3. I will make sure to provide time after a peer feedback session for students to reflect not only on the feedback they received but also to think about—and perhaps even share whole class—what went well and what could be improved.

5 Creating a Game Plan

Implementing Teacher and Peer Feedback

MY STORY

As a writer, I welcome feedback to make my stories better. While the actual act of writing is usually done alone, the quality of our writing improves substantially when we are open to feedback. Even when we continue to revise our work on our own and read it aloud to hear how it sounds, we still need to know how our writing sits with readers. After all, since we are writing for an audience, we need to know what others think of our work.

I believe that we should listen carefully to, and take notes on, all feedback that someone takes the time to share with us. But then what? How do we act on feedback? What feedback should we implement right away, what should we set aside for later, and what might we decide to ignore? Perhaps we should treat feedback as a buffet meal, considering all the options and then choosing what we want. Like a buffet, however, we may not know, at first, what we like. We may choose something, and then, after trying it, decide we don't really like it. And we may go back to the buffet for something that we didn't originally choose. Following this analogy, I carefully consider all feedback provided by my critique partners, agent, and editors. Some I gobble up right away and implement; some I may need to think about a bit longer to decide if I want to taste and try it out; and some I consider but eventually scrape off my plate and discard. Knowing our goals well helps inform the feedback that we'll implement. At a buffet, we may have a goal of wanting to eat healthy, avoiding gluten, or stocking up on protein. Those goals will inform what foods we put on our plate. We may still be open to some options outside of those food choices though. Similarly, if we have a writing goal of adding more details, we'll want to implement feedback related to that, but we'll also likely be open to other kinds of feedback that will make our writing better.

Before we turn to how we help students implement feedback on their goals, let me give you a couple of examples of how I made decisions about what feedback to implement in my own writing and how, ultimately, that feedback made my stories stronger.

Let's Dance! is the first book I published in 2020. It's a picture book about dances from around the world and the diverse children who enjoy them. In the original draft, I wrote a refrain that appeared twice in each stanza: "I love to dance." A writer-friend, who was serving as my only critique partner at the time, suggested that I delete that line throughout the story because she didn't think it was necessary. She also pointed out a stanza at the end of the first page: "I love to dance!/Tappity-tap./I love to dance!/Fingers snap." She suggested starting with those words, minus the words "I love to dance." She said if I did that, my story would immediately get people dancing. I took her advice on both accounts.

Less than a year later, I sold that revised manuscript. I was so thrilled that this would be my first book, and I made it very clear to the editor that I wanted the illustrations to represent children from diverse backgrounds. Fortunately, the editor shared my vision. Since I submitted the manuscript without illustration notes throughout—originally, I only included a note for the illustrator on the last page—my editor asked me to write the name of each dance that the words I'd written were describing. She was pleased with what I provided, but three months later, she reached out to me, saying that she had an idea. She said that my words could be matched to cultural dances. For instance, I had pictured tap dance for the words "Tappity-tap/Fingers snap," but my editor said those words could also describe flamenco dance. While I initially envisioned "Glide and slide/Side to side" as the Electric Slide or Cha Cha Slide, she said those words could describe Chinese long sleeve dancing. I was so thrilled that my editor had elevated my vision for a book that would feature children from different backgrounds.

As you can see in Figure 5.1, I immediately implemented the suggestions I was given by my friend and editor. I had no doubt that they would make my story better, and both of the suggestions were aligned with my intention: to create a story that readers would love and to highlight children who aren't often seen in books.

We don't always receive feedback that resonates with us, however. This was the case with another manuscript. *The March for Hope* is a picture book I wrote about a girl and her mother who attend the 2017 Women's March, and an awakening the young girl has while there. On the day prior to the march, the girl experiences something at school that remains on her mind throughout the day as she marches alongside her mother. It is something so distressing and confusing to the girl that she has not even told her mother about it. At the march, however, she feels inspired to share the story with her mother, revealing how she was mistreated by a teacher. The teacher's actions, though painful, become the catalyst for the girl's change. When I submitted this manuscript to a publisher,

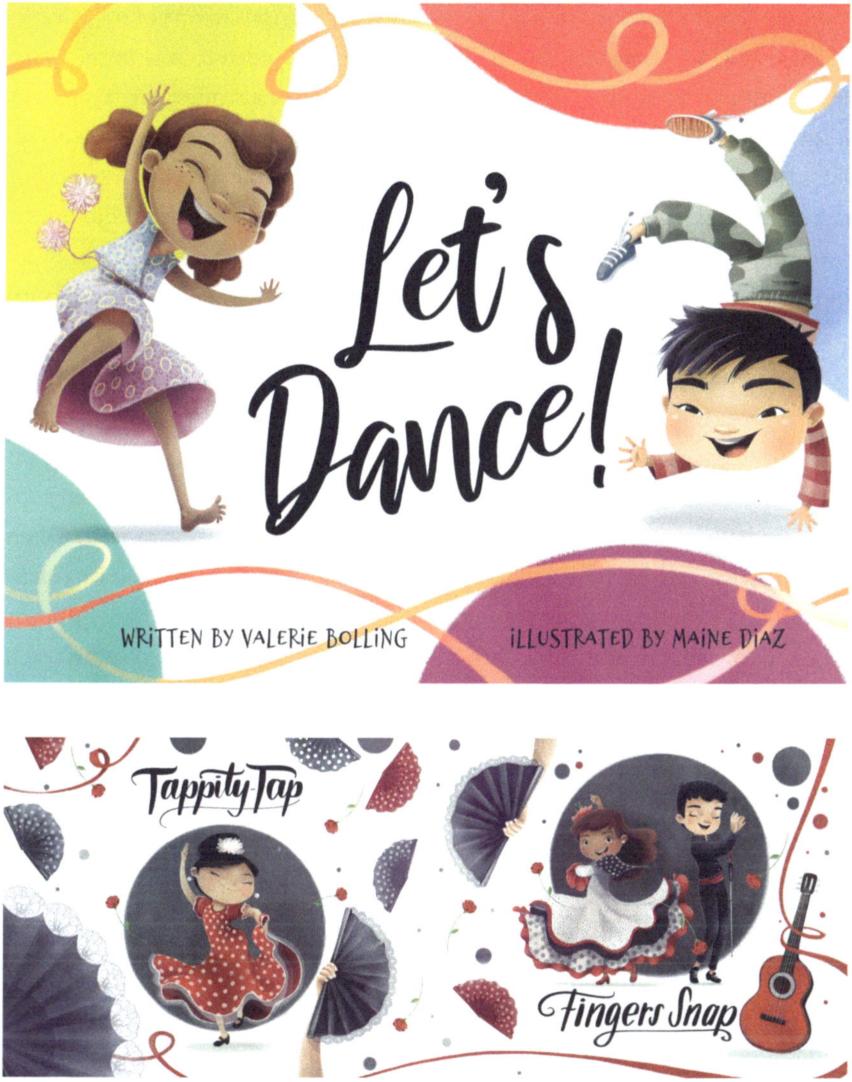

FIGURE 5.1 The cover of my first published book, *Let's Dance!* (top) and the spread inside the book that were influenced by feedback from a trusted critique partner and my editor (bottom)

the editor asked me to do an R&R—revise and resubmit—for the story and requested that I remove the teacher from the story altogether.

That feedback definitely didn't sit well with me. I made other revisions to the story that made it stronger, but I felt that the teacher was crucial to the story. However, because I wanted to keep an open mind, I did write a version of the story in which I removed the teacher. I read both versions to one of my critique groups, and every member agreed that the teacher needed to stay in the story. Since I didn't revise the story according to the editor's request, my agent was hesitant to send the revised manuscript to her. However, I asked him to do so, because I knew the story had gotten stronger as a result of other suggestions the editor had made, which I did implement, and other work that I did on my own simply because I was in revision mode. In the end, that editor not only acquired the manuscript but said she wanted even more "connective tissue" with the teacher.

One of the most valuable lessons we can teach students is to be true to themselves as writers. When students, and people, in general, honor themselves and what really matters to them, they will write better stories and make progress on their goals. Beyond teaching students how to receive feedback, we can support students' agency in the feedback implementation process as well. Often students assume they have to implement all feedback given to them by teachers or peers, whether it resonates with them or not. But if we want to support students' ownership of their goals and keep them meaningful, we need to teach them how to select which feedback to implement and make a plan for how they'll do that.

The stories I've shared thus far in this chapter have all involved me giving my story over to someone and having them provide whatever feedback they felt was appropriate. While this is valuable at times, it's even more productive if writers request what type of specific feedback they'd like. Of course, it's good to be open to feedback beyond what you ask for, but teaching students to be specific about what they want allows them agency in the process. It also provides space for them to think critically about what would benefit them the most as goal-setters and writers.

When I meet with my critique groups, I often tell them a specific part of the story that I'd like for them to focus on. For instance, since I know how important it is to grab the reader at the beginning of the story, there are times when I want my critique partners to provide feedback just on that part. I'll write several beginnings and ask for feedback about which one works best and why. Yes, there may be other parts of the story that could use work as well, but in that moment, I want my critique group to focus on just one part of the story. In another meeting, I may want feedback on how to make the language more lyrical or how to pick up the pacing. Since students have already created goals by the time they meet with feedback partners, it's easy for them to ask a peer or you to focus on how they're progressing toward a particular goal.

Thinking back to the buffet analogy, what's great about implementing feedback is that we can always put something aside—leave it on our plate—and try something else. Teaching students how to implement feedback on their goal progress is more than just holding them accountable for making revisions and getting work done. It is also teaching them that implementing feedback is about making choices, trying out new ideas, and choosing what makes sense to them as the creator of their goals.

WHY IT'S IMPORTANT TO PROVIDE A SPACE FOR IMPLEMENTING GOAL FEEDBACK

If students set goals, apply these goals to their writing, and receive feedback on their writing from peers and teachers, then it's important that they have the opportunity to implement the feedback they've received. This implementation step is an integral part of the goal-setting process. As Brookhart writes, "Feedback can lead to learning only if the students have opportunities to use it. One of the best ways you can help students learn to use feedback is to make sure you build in opportunities for students to use it fairly soon after they receive it" (2008, 73).

Just as it's important for students to choose their goals, they must also have the opportunity to choose what feedback they will implement. They don't have to include all of it, but they need to make thoughtful decisions about the feedback they'll use to make their writing better and to make progress toward their goals.

We all receive feedback often in our lives, whether we've asked for it or not. Therefore, you might invite students to think beyond their writing, and ask them where they receive feedback elsewhere in their lives and how they decide what to pay attention to. For example, a baseball player may get feedback about needing to run faster between bases or working harder to catch fly balls in the outfield. However, if that player's goal is to work on her batting, then she will be more interested in feedback that helps her hit harder and farther when she's up at bat. Another student may be a musical theater performer and get feedback about needing to work on his dance moves, but if that student's current goal is to become a better singer, he will prefer to get feedback related to how he can improve his vocal range. Whenever you can help students think about how they can transfer what they are doing with their writing goals to other aspects of their lives (and vice versa), take the opportunity to do so.

Deciding what feedback to implement requires thoughtfulness, maturity, and both critical and creative thinking. Students must determine what feedback is essential, what feedback might be worth trying out, and what feedback can be ignored. Once you and their peers have provided feedback, it's up to them to decide what to do with that feedback. They will have agency over their own work and decisions.

Not all students will know how to decide what feedback to implement and what they may choose to forgo, so they will need tips and instruction from you to help them with this process. In her article, "Students and Goal Setting: My Choice, My Growth, My Responsibility," teacher Betsy Hubbard reflects on the ways she supports her third graders with learning to make these important decisions about implementing feedback in their writing.

> *When I am conferring with students I am able to coach and guide students in their decision making. This is one more way I can give students a choice within [writing] workshop with support. It is also an opportunity for students to be thoughtful and reflective within their process, a skill that carries beyond writing (Hubbard 2016).*

Just as students have selected the goals they are working on, they will select the feedback they want to implement. Since it can be tough to decide what feedback to implement, below are some tips to help you provide a space for implementing feedback and guide students through the process.

FIVE TIPS TO HELP STUDENTS CHOOSE WHAT FEEDBACK TO IMPLEMENT IN THEIR WRITING

1. **Stay Focused on Your Goals.** Some feedback, like that related to grammar and mechanics, is fairly straightforward. There's often no decision to make; it just needs to be implemented. With other feedback, however,

it can be challenging to know if the suggested changes should be implemented and, if so, how. If you encourage students to stay focused on their goals, this process will be more manageable. There should never be an expectation to implement *all* feedback, but, as I said earlier, all feedback should be *considered*. When you advise students to stay focused on their goals, and carefully consider the comments related to their goals, they will be able to make decisions about what feedback to implement more effectively and efficiently.

2. **Look at Past Assignments.** It's a good idea for students to look at past assignments to see what feedback they've received. If they've received feedback, from either a peer or you, that is similar to advice they received in the past, that may be feedback worth implementing. For example, if a student has previously been given feedback about writing a stronger conclusion, and is getting similar feedback again, that's a sign that this may be an area on which to focus. It can be particularly helpful for students to look back at previous assignments in which they had to select a goal to focus on and write it at the top of their paper. They can review feedback on these assignments (as well as any reflections they've written about past goals) and consider if this helps them choose which feedback to implement on a current assignment. This looking-back process helps students see patterns in their writing. A student working on writing strong conclusions may not become excellent at this skill overnight but is likely to improve on this skill if she works on it across several assignments.

   Often in school, and life, we chip away at a goal over time, so continuing to consider and implement feedback related to a goal we've been working on for a while is often a productive choice. Since we do so many things "in the moment," it can be helpful to take some time away from a piece of writing, and then go back and read over what we were thinking at the time. Looking back at past assignments to see what they did to work on their goals, and what feedback they received, can help students determine what feedback they should implement related to those goals.

3. **Look at Feedback Notes.** I mentioned that during the peer feedback process, students must be required to take notes. These notes are an integral part of the goal-setting and revision process. Students will return to these notes, hopefully, again and again. Even if at the time the feedback

was given it made sense, it may not be as clear to them when they return to it later. If students have taken careful notes, what they've jotted down will be helpful to them as they begin to think about what feedback to implement and how to do it. If their notes aren't clear, which can certainly happen, encourage students to check in with you and/or their feedback partner—whoever provided the feedback—to seek clarification. They shouldn't ignore feedback that they don't understand; they should ask about it. After all, it could be worthwhile feedback that they'll want to implement.

4. **Take Time to Reflect.** Now that students have looked at past assignments and their notes on the current assignment, provide time for them to reflect. Before students dive into implementing feedback, it's important that they review their feedback notes and any other notes that they've taken during this process. This is a time to check again to make sure that they understand all of the feedback and that they've selected the feedback specifically related to their goals. Perhaps they may want to use highlighters to color code feedback. Perhaps they'll use one color to code feedback related to their goals and another color for feedback that they plan to implement, even if it's not directly related to their goals. Though feedback related to goals is the focus, there's likely other feedback worth implementing as well. Thus, while you'll instruct students to focus on feedback related to their goals, you'll also want to remind them that goal-related feedback isn't the only feedback they should implement.
5. **Make a Plan.** Sometimes looking at all of the feedback, and the notes related to the feedback, can be overwhelming. Therefore, it can be helpful to suggest that students make a plan for implementing their feedback. You may even give them a graphic organizer to assist with this. This plan can be done in different ways. Students could write down the type of feedback that they will implement first. For example, they may want to focus on feedback related to a particular goal. Students may also decide to work on a particular part of the assignment first. For instance, if they know they need a stronger beginning or introduction, they may choose to start there. This plan could also include what they will work on each day, or during each class, so they don't feel they have to work on everything at once. If we go back to the buffet analogy that I mentioned

Feedback Implementation Planning Form

Name: ______________________________ Date: __________

My goal:

____

____

____

What feedback have I received on this assignment?

____

____

____

____

Have I received any similar or related feedback on previous assignments?

____

____

What feedback will I implement in this assignment?

____

____

____

What feedback will I implement first?

____

____

What feedback will I save for another time or choose not to implement?

____

____

FIGURE 5.2 Feedback Implementation Planning Form

earlier in the chapter, we don't necessarily have to try everything at once. Students can use the form in Figure 5.2 (Appendix I) to help them record and reflect upon feedback and decide what they want to implement.

Some students may find it helpful to check in with their accountability partner or write a plan on their calendar to keep them on track with their feedback implementation. They may also want to refer to some of the tools introduced in Chapter 3 to see if another tip may help them stay on track with implementing feedback.

SAMPLE LESSON: PLANNING FOR STUDENT-LED TEACHER CONFERENCES

Note: Student/teacher conferences can be held at any point during the writing process. This sample lesson, however, provides an opportunity for students to discuss and provide examples of what feedback they chose to implement in their writing as well as what feedback they may have chosen to ignore. (The feedback referred to in this lesson includes notes from you as well as from their peers.) Students will justify their decisions and also connect these decisions to their goals. Though this lesson relates to writing goals, this approach can also be used for other goals. Teaching students how to decide what feedback is valuable versus what can be ignored, and providing a space for implementing the feedback that will help them with their goals, is a valuable lesson.

Model Ask your students if one of them would be willing to "star" in a video or do a live session to demonstrate a student/teacher conference. Alternatively, you can record yourself and another teacher having a conference with one of you playing the role of the student. Tell students that they will be detectives as they watch the video (or the live session) to note what they see happening. Be sure to set time aside to prep in advance and do a practice run. Once the video is ready, or you're ready for the live performance, you may do this lesson.

At the start, you'll tell your students that they will be detectives as they watch the student/teacher conference, paying careful attention to what they notice. You'll want to provide some questions for them to think about and jot some notes. It's possible you may want to create a handout for students to record their thinking as they watch the student/teacher conference. Some questions you might ask students to consider are:

- Who's leading the conference?
- What is the student saying about what feedback was implemented, what wasn't, and why?
- What is the student saying about how the feedback implementation choices are related to their goals?
- How is the teacher responding?

- Who's taking notes during the conference? (Hopefully, both are, so you'll want to be sure this is shown in the video or live model.)
- What questions do you have for the student and/or teacher?
- What will you take away from this conference to be sure you do in your own conference?

Respond Ask students what they notice. They may respond to some of the questions above with a partner, in small groups, or with the whole class.

Try It Presumably, this lesson is being done before you schedule conferences with each of your students. Therefore, students should focus on reviewing the piece of writing they'll talk about with you. They should look at some feedback they've already implemented and how it relates to their goal. To "try it out," students may share this information with a partner.

Questions Ask students if they have any questions and/or ask them how it felt to engage in this activity.

Do It Students should continue the work of preparing for their conference. They should look at the feedback they implemented, the feedback they ignored, and be prepared to discuss how they made their decisions. They should also be able to link the feedback they implemented, or didn't, to their goals. Since part of planning for a conference is preparing questions, students should write questions that they'd like to ask you, especially if they have questions about how they can better achieve their goals.

Share Ask students to share. Here are some questions they might respond to:

- What was easy or difficult about planning for your conference?
- Are you excited about your upcoming conference, or do you have questions or concerns about it?
- What can you do before your conference to make sure you're prepared?

Reflect Ask students to reflect upon the following questions. What will they take away from this lesson to apply to their student/teacher conference? What can they take from the lesson to transfer to another class or situation?

REFLECT AND SET YOUR OWN GOALS

Think about the type of feedback you provide students.

- Do you present it in a way that provides them with options?
- Do you tell them how they should "fix" something, or do you provide space for them to determine how to revise?
- How do you hold students accountable to reflect upon feedback you and their peers provide and decide which feedback they will implement?

Set a goal for how you will make space for students to have more agency in implementing the feedback they receive.

Examples:

1. When providing feedback, I will use language that provides options for students, perhaps asking questions instead of making statements.
2. I will ask students to reflect on the feedback they have received and choose what they will implement, and what they will ignore, and why.
3. I will plan lessons that help students determine what feedback is aligned with their goals and how to ask for feedback that helps them achieve their goals.

6 Checking in on the Game Plan

Guiding Students to Monitor and Assess Goal Progress

MY STORY

For the first few years that my husband, Sheldon, and I created New Year's goals, we didn't look back at them again until a year later, on the following New Year's Eve. We assessed our goals to see what we had accomplished both to celebrate our successes and determine what goals we might want to carry forward to the following year. Of course, we added new goals each year as well.

After a few years of doing this, we realized that waiting an entire year to check in on our progress wasn't the best plan to move forward with our goals. Sometimes, we had even forgotten a particular goal, which means that we certainly hadn't been working on it throughout the year. After recognizing that our goal-setting process wasn't as effective as it could be, I suggested that we should check in on our goals mid-year, so we began to check in on our goals each summer. That was a perfect check-in time for us; summer is a mid-year point, and as teachers, we had the summer off. In those summer months, we checked in to see where we both were with working toward our goals and had time to commit more strongly to those goals that we may not have focused diligently on during the first part of the year.

Having this mid-year check-in was beneficial, but as we continued to work on goals, we realized that checking in more frequently would benefit us even more. These check-ins would help keep our goals at the forefront of our minds and motivate us to work toward them. After all, when I did goal-setting work with my students, I didn't wait until the end of the year to have them check in on their goals. Though I did have my students check in mid-year, I also had them check in much more frequently throughout the year. As you can see with the number of instructional activities I've mentioned in this book, students checked in with peers on their goals—with both accountability and feedback partners; they checked in with me during student/teacher conferences; and they were required to target and reflect on particular goals in certain assignments. It seemed that if I was asking my students to check in more consistently on their goals, then Sheldon and I should do the same.

As teachers, Sheldon and I tend to make plans with the school calendar in mind. Since we're fortunate enough to have a week off for winter and spring breaks, we decided to check in on our goals during those times as well. Sometimes I even try to have us check in monthly, but we don't always manage to do that. The fact that we are checking in on our goals at least four times throughout the year, instead of only once, is certainly an improvement on our early years of goal setting. We are able to realize sooner when we haven't been working earnestly on a goal, and we are also able to reflect on and discuss if we should adjust a goal or choose a different one. What's best is that when we realize we've been making really good progress on a goal, we can celebrate it earlier instead of waiting until the end of the year or the beginning of the next one. Celebrating goal accomplishments, which I'll talk more about in Chapters 7 and 8, is also an important part of the goal-setting process.

WHY IT'S IMPORTANT FOR STUDENTS TO MONITOR THEIR GOALS

If students set goals, apply these goals to their writing, and receive and implement feedback from peers and teachers, then monitoring their actual progress toward their goals is essential. After all, if they miss this crucial step of the goal-setting process, how will they know what progress they're making? Chase Nordengren writes:

> *In order to make goals successful, students need consistent opportunities to revisit their goal, monitor progress, and understand opportunities for further growth. They also need the positive reinforcement that comes from seeing their effort pay off: the opportunity to celebrate success (2022, 65).*

When students monitor their goals, they can take pride in their achievements and also figure out where they may need to make adjustments. Perhaps they've made such significant progress on a particular goal that they can add another one in its place. Or there might be a goal that they haven't made much progress on, and they can think about why that may be. Maybe there's a goal that needs to be changed entirely or perhaps it's just the strategies that need to change. You can suggest that students revisit some of the tips shared in Chapter 3—like writing some action steps on a calendar or checking in with an accountability partner—to help them proceed more successfully toward their goals. Assessing where we are with our goals keeps us focused on making progress toward them.

When students assess how they're progressing toward their goals, this is truly an act of independence and agency. Students are doing the work of looking at the goals they selected to see how they're making strides toward achieving them. They are determining whether they're being successful with their goals or not. Yes, they will use evidence and data to make their decisions, which I'll talk about later in the chapter, but, ultimately, it is they themselves who will decide whether to adjust their goals or strategies, add a new goal, or shout with glee that they have already achieved one of their goals.

When you afford students the time to take stock of all of the writing they've done and monitor the growth they've made regarding their goals, they will see the purpose of goal setting and the connection between this work and their growth. This monitoring step is also important because students sometimes believe that the tasks assigned in school are busy work and/or irrelevant to their lives. In other words, if you are going to do this goal-setting work with your students, then you must provide time for them to monitor their progress toward goals frequently, so that it is a valuable learning experience. Students will then be able to see that the instruction you plan for them, and the assignments they do related to this instruction, are indeed worth their time. Moreover, it keeps their goals at the forefront of their minds. At any point in the school year, you could ask my students what their goals were, and they could tell you without having to look at their Goal Setting Organizer because they worked on them consistently. The same is true for my husband and me. We always know what our goals are. If students have to look at the page or digital document where they wrote down their goals to remember what they are, it may mean you're not providing sufficient opportunities for them to work on them and assess their progress.

Another aspect of checking in on goal progress is that it provides another chance for you to remind students to look at how they may have worked on these goals in another class, and what evidence might support that. You can prompt students to take some time to monitor goals they may set in places outside of writing—perhaps connected to improving their behavior, sports performance, or even developing or strengthening a family relationship. As I've mentioned before, any time that you can apply goal setting to other parts of students' lives, take the opportunity to do so.

Moreover, assessing goals can be an enjoyable process for both teachers and students alike. I remember that when my students reflected on their progress, it was always a special time in my classroom. Though it was wonderful for me to see the progress my students made—and to have parents tell me how they'd seen their children grow as writers in my class—what brought me the most joy was when students themselves noticed and were proud of the progress that they'd made.

HOW YOU CAN HELP STUDENTS MONITOR THEIR GOALS

In my English classroom, I would begin this goal-monitoring process by "hyping it up," letting students know what a fabulous opportunity this would be for them to check in, notice, and celebrate the progress they'd made on their goals. I'd say something like: "You've been working hard on your goals this year and have made progress as writers. I'm proud of you, and I want you to enjoy this time looking at evidence of your own progress. I guarantee you'll be proud of yourselves, too."

This may even be a good time for you to share your own goals and the progress you've made. (Feel free to share the ones you set at the end of Chapter 1 or even at the end of another chapter.) You might even model some of the steps below for students, using your own goals. Allowing students to get an inside look at how you use evidence to reflect on how you've been working on your goals and how you'll determine your next steps will provide guidance for them as they go through the process. This could also be a good time to show them how they might track their progress in an organizer or calendar. Again, you can use your goals to model how to track progress. In the sample lesson at the end of this chapter, I provide ideas for how you might model this process for students.

FIVE STEPS FOR MONITORING AND ASSESSING PROGRESS ON STUDENT GOALS

1. **Provide Time.** The most important thing you can do is provide time for students to monitor their goals. Making time to do this exemplifies that it's valuable, and it also guarantees that it will happen. If you simply suggest that students monitor their goals, but don't make time to do so, it probably won't happen. Think about the example with my husband and myself. We monitor our goals at specific times of the year. We know when we'll monitor our goals, and that's when we do it. We don't generally think about other times to check in beyond the times we've already set aside. And how do we remember to check on our goals? Since it's a part of our annual routine, we know the times we'll either create new goals or check in on our progress. We also put dates on our calendar to remind

ourselves to check in during school breaks. Therefore, I suggest that you write in your teaching plans the times when you'll want students to monitor their goals and plan the lessons that will guide them in doing so. You'll likely want to set aside more than one day for this work, and will want to teach more than one monitoring lesson, especially the first time students engage in this work. Once the time has been set aside, then you can decide on and plan the specific lessons you'll teach.

2. **Look at the Evidence.** You'll need to provide explicit instruction for how students should go about assessing their goal progress. You can start by asking students to gather multiple pieces of evidence, or data, to help them monitor their goals. Reviewing graded assignments and assessments, self-reflections, and peer and teacher feedback will give them a picture of how they've been progressing toward their goals. It would be a good idea to model what this process should look like because it could be overwhelming for students to have a number of assignments and notes ready to go but not know exactly how to analyze them to determine their progress. For example, if a student has been working on a goal of writing engaging introductory paragraphs, they might gather assignments where they tried that out, some peer feedback they received on this goal, as well as a draft where they were brainstorming several possible openings for an essay. The evidence students gather will depend a bit on what their goal is, but if they've truly been working on this goal, they should have several pieces of evidence to pull from. You can offer students several suggestions to make this process manageable and effective.

   In order to make this process feel accessible and not overwhelming, you might limit the pieces of evidence you recommend students review. For example, you might ask them to look at three assignments. You may further advise that students choose an assignment from the beginning of the year, one a month or more later, and their most recent assignment. Alternatively, you could also require students to look at two assignments, one from earlier in the year and one more recent, as well as a self-reflection they wrote. Offering students a limited scope with options will help them. If you have some students who are more ambitious and can handle looking at more work samples to determine their progress, you should allow them to do that.

Providing students with an organizer to track their progress, like the one in Figure 6.1 (Appendix J), would also be helpful. There should be space for students to list their goals and the accompanying evidence. For each piece of evidence, there should be a space to comment on how they worked on the goal in the piece. (This information can come from what they currently observe, their self-reflection notes, or written comments—including direct quotes made by you or a peer.) They should also note either what more they could have done to work on the goal or what their next steps will be.

Another idea, which may be beneficial for students to process this monitoring of their goals, is to work with their accountability partner. In their book, *Teaching Students to Drive Their Learning*, Douglas Fisher, Nancy Frey, Sarah Ortega, and John Hattie write about the power of student collaboration as it relates to monitoring goal progress. "Students working in pairs or small groups must learn to listen carefully, consider

Goal Monitoring Form

Name: ______________________ Date: __________

Goal 1:

Progress I've Made Toward My Goal

____

____

Evidence (List at least three pieces of evidence from your writing.)

1. ____

   ____

2. ____

   ____

3. ____

   ____

Next Steps/What I Want to Continue to Do/Something New I Will Do

____

____

FIGURE 6.1 Goal Monitoring Form

the ideas of others, present their own, and come to consensus" (2023, 102). Though monitoring one's goals is a self-reflective process that is generally done individually, some students may benefit from being able to talk with another person about this process. For example, when my husband and I check in on our goals, we do it together. We discuss what we accomplished and what we might do next, and we are able to give each other feedback. I might think of another way Sheldon worked on a particular goal that he didn't remember, and he might give me a suggestion for something I could do to work more on a particular goal.

When students chat with a peer during this process, they can gain similarly helpful information. For some students, checking in with a peer may even mean that their peer can help them organize and understand their evidence. For students who may need more help, you may want to offer them guided instruction in a small group or even meet with them one-on-one. The hope is that if you coach them through the goal-monitoring process the first time, they will be able to do it on their own, or with less guidance, the next time. While some students may appreciate the opportunity to talk through, with a peer, what they notice about their goal progress, others may prefer to do this work on their own. It's up to you if you want to have everyone experience this peer conversation the first time they monitor their goals or if you'll make it optional. If you have all of your students participate in the peer exchange, then moving forward, you can let students decide whether they prefer to have some time to discuss their evidence and progress toward goals with a peer or if doing it independently works best for them. Figure 6.2 (Appendix K) shows a chart you might give students to help scaffold these peer conversations.

Ways to Help a Classmate Monitor Goals

- "Where did you find evidence of working toward your goal?"
- "One way I notice you working toward your goal is [name evidence]."
- "Will you continue to work on this goal in this unit, or will you set a new goal?"

FIGURE 6.2 Ways to Help a Classmate Monitor Their Goal

3. **Provide a Check-in Chart.** Charts and graphic organizers can be very helpful to students. If your students used the Goal Setting Organizer in Chapter 2 (Figure 2.2), that's a good place to start because they'll know their check-in dates. During the check-ins, you can provide students with questions they can respond to, such as the ones in Figure 6.2. If you want to create a checklist for students to use, feel free to do so, but I believe it's always a good idea to require students to do more than just mark a check next to a list of items. They should write a couple of sentences with specific examples, explaining why they did or didn't mark a check.
4. **Reflect and Decide on Next Steps.** Once students have monitored their work and assessed where they are, they need time to reflect. They may have already noted what they will continue to work on related to their goals, or what their next steps might be, as they've looked at each piece of evidence. They still need time, however, to look at all of the feedback they've received on their assignments, not just those related to their goals. Fisher, Frey, Ortega, and Hattie emphasize that, "monitoring progress requires that we learn to ask ourselves questions. We must develop the skills of reflecting and using information to determine whether we are meeting our goals" (2023, 93). Of course, students will have their own thoughts about what they'd like to reflect on, but it could be helpful to provide them with questions to guide their thinking. You might ask them to think about the following questions:

    - What are the goals and strategies where I'm experiencing the greatest success, and why?
    - What are the goals and strategies where I'm having difficulty, and why?
    - Would I like to switch out one of my goals for another?
    - Would I like to change any of my strategies?
    - Is there an action step I can take to make further progress on my goals? (Example: Check in more frequently with an accountability partner.)

    These questions are simply ideas. I don't intend for you to require students to respond to all of them, and you will surely have some questions of your own that will make sense for your students to think about.

You may even want students to reflect on the goal-monitoring process itself. How did it work for them? What might they do differently next time? This could be a good time for students to think about what aspects of the process worked best for them. For instance, if you had them check in with an accountability partner, was that helpful to them, or would they have preferred to work on their own? If you provided a number of options for goal-progress charts, which one worked best for them, or would they like to design one of their own? For students who worked with you either in a small group or one-on-one, it would be very useful for them to reflect upon that process and to think about if they'd be able to work on their own next time or have less support. Here are some other questions you might offer students to reflect on:

- What do I most want to remember about this experience to incorporate the next time I monitor my goals?
- How can I take something from this experience and apply it to another subject or part of my life? (Note: This might be a good time for students to monitor their progress in another area. What evidence might they look at to see how they've become a better reader, athlete, or artist?)
- What feedback do I have for my teacher about how this process worked?

5. **Celebrate.** Progress toward goals definitely needs to be celebrated! Though I will talk more about end-of-year celebrations in Chapter 8, students should be given the opportunity to celebrate their progress during this monitoring part of the process. You and your students can decide if they'll share their accomplishments with an accountability partner, with the whole class, or just with you. You might ask students to write a letter or email to their parent(s) or caregiver(s) about their progress. This should be short; if you require them to write too much, it won't seem like a celebration. Students can share just one or two things that they are most proud of about their goal progress, and give an example or two. These examples can come straight from their goal-monitoring chart. You could also plan some sort of whole-class celebration as part of this process.

SAMPLE LESSON: LOOKING AT EVIDENCE TO MONITOR PROGRESS TOWARD GOALS

Model You can begin the lesson by asking students, "Why do you think it's important to monitor our goals?" or by telling them, "It's important to monitor our goals to make sure we're on track and to see if there are changes we can make now to have even more success." Next, you can proceed by showing students how to review their progress toward their goals by looking at evidence—such as assignments, assessments, teacher and peer feedback, and any other data that may be useful—to see how they've improved.

To teach this explicitly, you'll need to have a sample goal clearly displayed as well as accompanying pieces of evidence. If you have a goal and evidence of your own to demonstrate this, you may use that; otherwise, you may want to use a student sample. If you're requiring students to use three pieces of evidence, you should use the same number as you model. If you choose to add another piece of evidence, it will be because you want to explain how students might use a different piece of evidence, and it will also serve as a model for students who want to push themselves to do more than the requirement. During this modeling process, you should not only share your thinking out loud, but also record the progress noted in the same chart (such as the one in Figure 6.1) that you expect students to use to show them how to record their own data.

Respond Ask students what they notice. They may discuss their observations with a partner, in small groups, or with the whole class.

Try It To make this lesson as efficient as possible, you should prepare students for the goal-monitoring process by telling them about it a day or two before, so that they have time to gather their evidence. Ask them to look at one piece of evidence to assess how they worked on a particular goal. You can either have them share that information verbally with a partner or ask them to write it down. If you've already given students a goal-monitoring chart and told them how to use it, they can write the information on their chart. However, if you are planning to teach a lesson in the future about recording evidence, they can still write down the information elsewhere for now.

Questions Ask students if they have any questions and/or how it felt to engage in this activity.

Do It Students should continue monitoring their goals, using the evidence they've selected. You may suggest that they work on one goal at a time, looking for examples of how they worked on that goal in different pieces of writing.

Share Ask students to share. Here are some questions they might respond to:

- What was easy about finding evidence for the work you've done on your goals?
- What was difficult about finding evidence for the work you've done on your goals?
- What did you learn about yourself and your goals?
- Was there anything that surprised you?
- Were there any patterns you noticed?

Reflect Give students the opportunity to reflect. How will they continue monitoring their goals when they return to this work in the next class? What can they take from the lesson to transfer to another class or situation?

REFLECT AND SET YOUR OWN GOALS

As you think about your students, consider the following questions.

- How might the goal-monitoring process support students in working toward and achieving goals?
- How can you build in time for students to monitor their goals?
- When can this be done individually, with a peer, or with you?

Set a goal for how you will build in time for students to monitor and reflect upon their progress throughout the year.

Examples:

1. I will write dates on my calendar when students will reflect upon their goals. (It could be at the end of a unit, before a marking period ends, or more frequently.)

2. As I plan lessons, I will think about which assignments may provide an ideal opportunity for students to monitor and reflect on how they worked on their goals.
3. I will give students parameters for when they can choose to reflect upon their goals, creating options within a certain time frame. (For example, instead of requiring that all students reflect on a particular date, I might say something like: "You need to check in on one of your goals during this unit or during this week." That offers students flexibility, especially if they'd like to look at a particular assignment as evidence. You know your students best, however, so you may prefer everyone to monitor their goals at the same time. If you go with the flexibility option, you'll likely need to provide reminders. Don't forget that even if you allow students flexibility on when they will monitor their goals, you still need to teach them how to do this work, making your expectations clear for how to go through the process and what they will need to do to complete it successfully.)

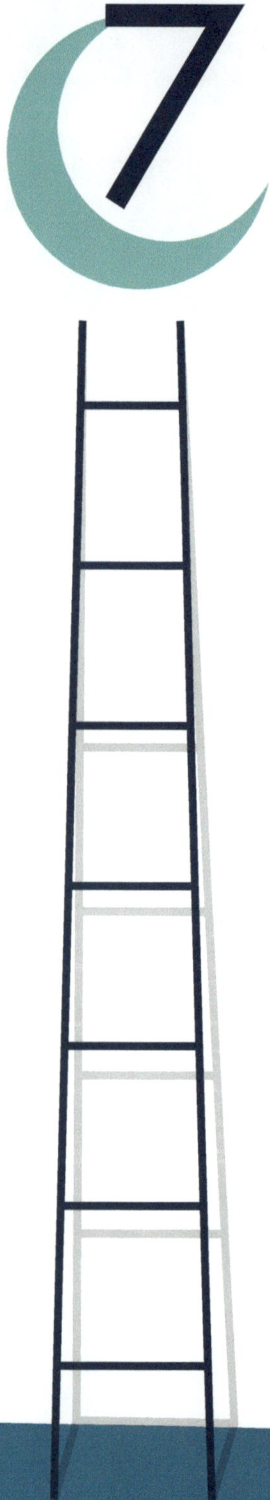

7 Time for a New Game Plan

Revising Goals

MY STORY

I know from personal experience that there are times when goals need to be revised. As you may remember, I write books for children. Though I have written articles about topics related to education, this is the first book I've written for teachers.

At the beginning of 2024, which is the year I began writing this book, these were the goals I had set for myself related to writing:

- Begin a genre study of middle grade books, particularly novels in verse (read novels in verse; look at middle grade book-writing tips in my files; and brainstorm story ideas).
- Explore the possibility of writing a professional book for Stenhouse Books.
- Keep promoting myself and my books in all ways possible (visiting schools, libraries, bookstores, festivals, and conferences; connecting with organizations and people who are good partners/collaborators; and posting regularly on social media).

Like most people, when I choose my goals, I intend to pursue them faithfully. However, by March, I realized that it would be best to revise my goals. I was in a number of spaces (conferences, festivals, and online discussions) where those of us who write for children were lamenting the reality that, in recent months, selling a book to a publisher was proving to be difficult. Therefore, I wasn't sure if it was the right time to forge ahead with my goal to write a middle grade novel. That doesn't mean I might not write one in the future, but making this my focus, at the time, no longer felt like the most worthwhile goal.

That said, in January, I had joined a group for middle grade writers and enjoyed attending their webinars. Although I put aside my strategies of reading middle grade novels and brainstorming story ideas, I stayed connected to the group and attended their sessions. After all, I could still dip my toes into my middle grade study goal, even if I wasn't diving in deeply.

On the other hand, though I thought I would just explore the idea of writing a professional book for teachers, I decided to commit to it. After all, unlike trying to sell one of my picture book manuscripts, I had an editor who was interested in having me write a book. It made sense to me to write for a publisher who wanted me to begin on a project immediately, as opposed to waiting to see if one of my other projects, pitched by my agent, would be acquired by a publisher.

My third goal has remained the same. I continue to promote my books as best I can, and I'm always looking for new opportunities and connections that will allow me to introduce my books to others. In particular, throughout the year, I followed up with a number of schools about arranging author visits, discovered new book festivals to attend, and connected with organizations interested in getting my books into the hands of young readers. I've also maintained a consistent social media presence.

It's important to make space for goals to change. Life is full of unexpected turns, and knowing we can revise our goals along the way is both realistic and reassuring. As 2024 progressed, I revised my goals to the following:

- Stay connected to the Middle Grade Writers Group, attending their sessions.
- Write a book for teachers about goal setting with Stenhouse Books.
- Keep promoting myself and my books in all ways possible (visiting schools, libraries, bookstores, festivals, and conferences; connecting with organizations and people who are good partners/collaborators; and posting regularly on social media).

As you can see, my first goal is the one that changed most significantly. Instead of trying to do a number of things related to middle grade writing, I chose only *one* thing that I felt I could reasonably accomplish by the end of the year. Of course, when I look at my goals later in the year, I may revise my middle grade goal again, realizing I can actually do more, like reading more middle grade books or even beginning to brainstorm ideas for my own story. My second goal became more specific. Instead of stating I'd *explore* writing a book, I said I'd *write it* and also named its subject matter. And you will notice that I didn't change anything at all about my last goal.

That's what's great about revising goals. Some goals change slightly; others change a lot; and there are those that don't change at all. The other thing I should point out is that, unlike what I've suggested you do with students, I didn't create strategies to achieve my goals because I've set goals for long enough that I intuitively know what actions and steps I plan to take in order to reach my goals. However, my first goal is a good example of how strategies might change.

I didn't even have the Middle Grade Writers Group listed in my original goal because I didn't know about it at the time, and yet that became the focus of my middle grade goal.

Fortunately, I enjoy revising—whether as part of the writing process or when reflecting upon my goals. I'm sure your students will enjoy this goal-revision process as well. It can be freeing to get rid of a goal that's not working, change strategies to make a goal work, and, of course, celebrate goals that have already been achieved before the end of the expected time frame.

WHY IT'S IMPORTANT FOR STUDENTS TO REVISE THEIR GOALS

If students set goals, apply these goals to their writing, and receive and implement feedback on their writing from peers and teachers, then having the opportunity to revise their goals is also an important part of the process.

Revision is a skill, and something we do in many different contexts. We revise our position at home plate, so our bat has a better chance of connecting with the ball. We revise how we deliver a line in a play to get a laugh from the audience. We revise our writing to make it more appealing to the reader. Goals, too, can be revised so that what we're striving for still makes sense for us, and we can continue to make progress.

When we afford students the time to revise their goals, we manifest that goals are flexible, that they can be changed. Chase Nordengren, in his book *Step into Student Goal Setting*, shares a story about a first-grade teacher who taught her students this valuable lesson early in their school career. "She [Courtney, the teacher]... highlights for students the opportunities they have to change their path to make their goal more accessible. 'If it doesn't work out the first time, what's your tool belt of strategies to help you either adjust the goal or achieve the goal?'" (2022, 33).

Not only can students think about strategies to help them adjust or achieve a goal, but they can also think about pushing a goal aside and choosing another one. I want students to enjoy this goal-setting process, which means giving them the opportunity to choose the goals they want to work on as well as those they may want to abandon or put on hold. Students might want to change a goal that they're no longer motivated by, or they may have discovered a new goal they'd prefer to work on. For example, a student may have had a goal related to including more text evidence in her essays but recently joined the school newspaper club and wants to focus on writing news articles. Maybe that student will instead create a specific goal of pitching three stories for the school newspaper. Adding appropriate text evidence to essays is still important, but going with a goal that motivates students—and over which they have agency—seems like a smart choice.

Just as I've shared goals that I revised and why, you might consider whether you've revised a goal (in any part of your life) and whether you'd like to share that experience with students. As your students revise their goals, remind and encourage them to look at goals they've set in another class or outside of school. They may want to revise some of those goals, too. The more you can invite students to apply the goal-setting process to other parts of their lives, the greater the chance that they'll begin to look for these opportunities and transfer these skills on their own. Another reason it might be important for students to revise goals is that continuing to work toward a goal that no longer feels reasonable, or that no longer works for you, is pretty demotivating—the opposite of what we want with goals! Making sure our goals are inspiring us to get to work—rather than dragging us down or making us want to avoid the task at hand—is paramount.

HOW YOU CAN HELP STUDENTS REVISE THEIR GOALS

To help your students with the process of revising their goals, it may be helpful for them to look at their goals through three lenses: 1) accomplished goals, 2) unsuccessful goals, and 3) goals where there's more to do. Within each category, you can provide a question and options for students to consider that will help them revise their goals. Let's explore what that looks like for each of these categories.

ACCOMPLISHED GOALS

- **Question:** Students should ask themselves, "How do I know I accomplished the goal?" This question is worth asking because if students can identify what they did that led to their success, then they might be able to apply that to other goals where they were unsuccessful or didn't make as much progress as they'd hoped.

- **Celebrate:** Achieving a goal is cause for a celebration! A celebration can be anything. It can be a victory dance. It can be doing something special with family. It can be adding names and goals to a "Wall or Hall of Achieved Goals". (You may recall that in Chapter 3, I suggested that you might create a "Wall or Hall of Tools" for students to share tools that are working for them. This is a similar concept.) In the next chapter, I'll provide more ideas for celebrating, but these are a few to get you started.
- **Choose another goal:** It's wonderful that students have accomplished a goal, but that doesn't mean they are done. Is there a way they can push further with that goal by taking the next step, or should they pick something else to work on?

UNSUCCESSFUL GOALS

- **Question:** Students should ask themselves, "Why do I think I was unsuccessful with this goal?" Just as it's important for students to recognize why they experienced success with a goal, it's also worth exploring why a goal wasn't achieved. If students can identify certain steps they could have taken that might have led to success, then perhaps they can recommit to the goal.
- **Make a change:** Sometimes the goal is worth keeping, but maybe one or more of the strategies should change. Perhaps a student chose a strategy that didn't work. For example, maybe a student said she would do grammar exercises related to commas three times a week but hasn't done that at all. Maybe another student planned to add more details to his work but realizes he hasn't taken time to go back into the text to find appropriate details to support his ideas. Could the first student change her strategy from doing exercises three times a week to once a week? Maybe doing the review with a caregiver or friend would be more successful for her. Perhaps the second student might decide to highlight important details and/or take notes as he reads, so that he can more easily find details to add to his work.
- **Abandon the goal:** Sometimes a goal may need to be abandoned entirely because it's just not working. The trick, however, is to know when it's okay to abandon the goal and when it's a goal that—even though it may be challenging—is still one worth pursuing. In other words, we don't want students to give up on a goal just because it's hard. After all, learning to do

hard things is a necessary part of life. However, if a student is really struggling with a goal and is unmotivated to work on it, perhaps it needs to be put aside for the time being. It can be substituted with another goal and may be revisited at another time.

MORE-TO-DO GOALS

- **Question:** Students should ask themselves, "What can I do to be more successful with this goal?" What's great about more-to-do goals is that students have made the decision to continue to work on a goal. They've realized that they haven't accomplished it yet, but they believe that with some adjustments, they can. They should take time to think about what might help them accomplish the goal. You may want to point students to the list of tools in Chapter 3 and your "Wall or Hall of Tools," if you have one.
- **Do something else first:** Sometimes students have chosen a goal that they think they can dive into, but they may need to do something else first. For example, the student who wants to use commas correctly may need to meet with you a time or two for a review of comma rules before doing comma exercises on her own. The student who wants to add more details to his writing may benefit from a lesson about choosing appropriate details for text evidence. This may be a lesson that would serve many of your students, or if you've already taught such a lesson, the student might need to confer with you, individually, for additional instruction or review.
- **Add more support:** Some students may need more support with their goals. A good question for them to ask themselves is: Are there other tools or support that could help me reach this goal? They may need to learn more about a particular topic; they may need more practice; or they may need to use another tool. Sometimes the support that students need is something they can do themselves. But sometimes this support involves another person. They may need to meet with their accountability partner more often, or they may need more check-ins with you. You may recall, from "My Story" in Chapter 1, that my check-ins with my editor at the beginning of writing this book were very helpful to me—and they continued to be instrumental throughout this book-writing process. When I got to a tricky part with writing, I knew I could count on her extra support to help me achieve my goal.

Goal Revision Organizer

Name: ______________________________ Date: __________

Revising our goals is an important part of the goal-setting process and can help us make greater progress toward achieving our goals. As you reflect upon your progress, use this organizer to determine the status of your goals, what revisions you'll make, and your next steps.

MY WRITING GOAL	STRATEGIES/ HOW I WILL WORK TOWARD MY GOAL	GOAL STATUS (CHECK ONE)	WHAT I'LL DO NEXT (CHECK ONE)	PLAN FOR MOVING FORWARD (WRITE A NEW/REVISED GOAL, NEW STRATEGIES, ETC.)
		☐ Accomplished ☐ Unsuccessful ☐ More-to-do	☐ I will set a new goal. ☐ I will abandon this goal. ☐ I will revise this goal. ☐ I will revise one or more strategies.	
		☐ Accomplished ☐ Unsuccessful ☐ More-to-do	☐ I will set a new goal. ☐ I will abandon this goal. ☐ I will revise this goal. ☐ I will revise one or more strategies.	
		☐ Accomplished ☐ Unsuccessful ☐ More-to-do	☐ I will set a new goal. ☐ I will abandon this goal. ☐ I will revise this goal. ☐ I will revise one or more strategies.	

FIGURE 7.1 Goal Revision Organizer

You might guide your students through this goal-revision process by using a Goal Revision Organizer like the one in Figure 7.1 (Appendix L). After filling out this form, you may want to give students a new Goal Setting Organizer (Figure 2.2 (Appendix B)) to record their updated goals. Some of the goals and strategies will be exactly the same, which is fine, but there will likely be one or more revised goals.

SAMPLE LESSON: REVISING GOALS TO ACHIEVE GREATER SUCCESS

Model You might start this lesson by reminding students why it's important to revise goals. You might say, "Revising our goals helps us stay on track and keeps us making progress toward what we want to accomplish." You could also ask students: "Why is revising goals important?"

Since revision is likely a normal part of the writing process in your classroom, students will be familiar with it. If students are used to monitoring their progress toward their goals, revision is an expected next step. In fact, some students may have already revised a goal or strategy during the monitoring process, or at other times when you've planned for reflection in class.

Depending on where your students are in their understanding of revision, you may be able to jump to the "Try It" part of the lesson, as you may not need much set-up beyond the introduction to the lesson and what you expect students to do. If your students would benefit from modeling, you can share a goal of yours and why and how you revised it. Even if you didn't revise a goal, you can imagine that you did, or you can share a sample from "My Story" at the beginning of the chapter.

Respond Ask students what they notice about the example you shared. They may discuss their observations with a partner, in small groups, or with the whole class.

Try It Ask students to take out their Goal Setting Organizer (Figure 2.1 or 2.2). For the "Try It," they should look at one of their goals and one of the accompanying strategies. They should think about if they've achieved the goal, if they should continue working on it, or if they've made little or no progress. Looking at any information they wrote during the monitoring process may also help them decide, if they're unsure. Once they decide what category the goal is in—accomplished, unsuccessful, or more-to-do—then they can decide if they should revise that goal or perhaps change a strategy. If they've achieved the goal, they can do a victory dance. They should record information about the first goal on their Goal Revision Organizer (Figure 7.1).

Questions Ask students if they have any questions and/or how it felt to engage in this activity.

Do It Students should continue looking at each of their goals and strategies, going through the process of determining which category each goal is in, and whether they need to revise any of their goals or strategies. They should continue to fill out the goal revision sheet as they work.

Share Ask students to share. Here are some questions they might respond to:

- Have you already achieved any of your goals? If so, what will you do to celebrate, and what new goal(s) will you put in its (their) place?
- Did you abandon any goals? If so, what wasn't working for you? How did you know you were ready to let that goal go?
- What about the more-to-do goals? Did you change or add any strategies? If so, why do you think these revised or new strategies will help you be more successful?

Reflect Ask students to reflect upon the following questions. How will they commit to their newly revised goals? What can they take from the lesson to transfer to another class or situation?

REFLECT AND SET YOUR OWN GOALS

Think about what you learned from your students as they worked on revising their goals.

- How can you build in time for students to revise their goals?
- When can this be done individually, with a peer, or with you?
- Are there any of your own goals that you may want to revise?

Set a goal for how you will build in time for students to reflect upon and revise their goals throughout the year.

Examples:

1. I will write dates on my calendar to plan for when students will reflect upon and revise their goals. (It could be at the end of a unit or quarter/semester/trimester. Minimally, it should happen mid-year; January is a good time to do this.)

2. As I plan lessons, I will provide time for students to reflect on their goals and consider what's working and what may not be, letting them know that if they're not making their desired progress, they may want to consider revising their goals or strategies. (This provides students with agency and not having to wait until you plan a goal-revision lesson.)
3. I will plan a lesson that allows my students and myself time to revisit the list of strategies we developed together (Figure 2.3) to see if there are other helpful strategies that could be added to the list. (This list of strategies was created when students first selected their goals. Now that they've been working on their goals, they may have new ideas to add. As you review your students' work, you might think of new strategies that could help them achieve success with their goals that you can add to the list.)

8 Scoring the Winning Goal!

Wrapping Up Goals and Moving Forward

MY STORY

As I've said earlier, my husband and I set goals at the beginning of each year, which include what we hope to achieve as individuals and as a couple. I also talked about how we check in on our goals throughout the year to see how we're progressing. We reflect on our goals at the end of each year—or at the beginning of the next one—and then create goals for the new year. We celebrate the goals we've achieved—by raising a glass of champagne at home or going out to dinner—and, for the ones we didn't accomplish, we decide whether we will carry those goals forward into the new year or leave them behind.

While I can't share how I reflected on my 2024 goals—as I write these words, it's still the middle of 2024—I can share how I used my 2023 Author Goals to inform the ones I set for 2024. In 2023, my goals were focused on finishing up a third revision of a chapter book and getting ready for my move to become a full-time author. I set goals to develop a proposal for an author-in-residence program to share on my website and emailed numerous schools with the goal of planning school visits for the 2023–2024 school year.

As I reflected on those goals at the end of the year, I was pleased to see how much work I'd done. I'd submitted the chapter book revisions to my agent; I'd added an author-in-residence program to my website (which I later changed to author/poet-in-residence program because a couple of schools were interested in a focus on poetry); and my efforts to reach out to schools resulted in a number of school visits. I celebrated those accomplishments, and they also informed my plan for moving forward.

Though I had submitted my chapter book revisions to my agent, we had other projects that were more of a priority to submit to editors, and we were still waiting to hear about a 2023 submission. Thus, for 2024, it meant that working on my chapter book was a goal I could put aside for the time being. I'd put so much work into revising the school visits and author/poet-in-residence program pages on my website—and to emailing and following up with schools—that I felt I could move away from that goal, too. I would still reach out to schools—and I would certainly respond to requests I received for school visits—but I didn't think I needed to put the same amount of time and energy into this endeavor as I had the previous year.

As I thought about the goals I wanted to set for 2024, I realized there were factors that had changed. Though I had retired after a thirty-year career as an educator and was excited to pursue my new career as a full-time author, the publishing industry for children's books had changed. It was becoming more and more challenging to have books acquired by publishers, and the wait time to hear from editors about their interest in manuscripts had significantly increased. Therefore, I decided that it might make sense to switch gears a bit. Instead of continuing to focus on writing picture books, I decided to investigate new genres. Therefore, one of my goals was to begin a study of middle grade books (even though I later revised that goal).

As you may remember, the editor of this book had reached out to me to write a book, and I decided to move forward with this offer. After all, it made sense for me to write a book for teachers; it was the perfect intersection of my passions for writing and teaching. Therefore, though my goal was to *explore* the possibility of writing a book for teachers, as evidenced by the book you're currently reading, it's clear that I did more than explore. I turned that goal into action by writing this book.

My final goal was to continue doing what I could to promote my books, including visits to schools, libraries, bookstores, book festivals, conferences, and connecting with organizations and people with whom it might be good to partner and collaborate. I decided to continue promoting my books and seeking opportunities, but I was more cognizant about which ones were most worth my time.

When deciding on new goals, it's not only important to consider our current goals but also what may have changed in our lives. Perhaps we have different priorities. Maybe there's a goal that seemed worthy of our focus, at the time, but then something else became more important. In my case, writing this book took precedence over my middle grade book study. Something in the world or in our family may have changed that requires a shift. Being retired from my career in education meant that I had more time available to do author visits at schools and other events, so I wanted to be sure I did what I could to facilitate that by updating my website with information about school visits. Goal setting and goal reflecting call for careful consideration and deep thought about ourselves and about other factors that may impact us.

WHY IT'S IMPORTANT FOR STUDENTS TO REFLECT ON THEIR GOALS AT THE END OF THE YEAR

Students have worked hard if they've set goals and worked on them all year. If they don't reflect on their progress at the end of school year, then the process would be incomplete. This reflection is important not only so that students can recognize what they've accomplished, but also to celebrate these accomplishments and make a plan for moving forward to experience even greater success in the future.

Part of this reflection should also include a plan for how students will move forward without you. They may not have a teacher next year who implements a goal-setting process, but that doesn't mean they can't set goals and continue to work on them. Perhaps they will stop by your classroom next year to let you know how they're doing with their goals. Maybe they will stay connected to their accountability partner and work on their goals together. They might bring a goal-setting process to their family members. As my husband and I do, they can provide support for each other with their goals and make goal setting part of their family tradition. Regardless of what each student ultimately decides to do to move forward, the three parts of this reflective process are:

1. Celebrate what you accomplished.
2. Decide what you will take away from this experience.
3. Make a plan for how you will move forward.

HOW YOU CAN HELP STUDENTS REFLECT ON THEIR GOALS AND CELEBRATE THEIR SUCCESSES

To help your students with the process of reflecting on their goals, it might be useful for them to look at their goals through three lenses as they did when revising their goals: accomplished goals, unsuccessful goals, and more-to-do goals. Let's take a look at how we might celebrate and determine takeaways from both the goals we accomplished and those for which there is still more work to do.

CELEBRATIONS

In *Celebrating Writers*, Ruth Ayres writes that, "celebration allows writers to revel in their personal writing process. It provides time for reflection and growth" (2013, 5). And there are so many ways to celebrate—individually, whole class, and outside of school. I'll share ideas for ways to celebrate at school, but I'm sure you and your students will have many other ideas. It could be fun to brainstorm a list of ideas with your students of different ways to celebrate. After creating the list together, you can then actually do one or more things on the list.

- **Create an Anthology of Student Writing:** Have each student submit a piece of writing to contribute to a class anthology, celebrating your class of authors and poets. You can publish the book electronically and/or make a printed copy for each student, perhaps with the help of a parent volunteer. You may decide to include students' artwork and videos, too.
- **Celebrate School-wide or by Grade Level:** If there's a school-wide focus on goal setting, perhaps there'll be a school-wide celebration. Even if the entire school isn't engaged in this process, you might plan for a grade-level celebration, if your colleagues have been partners with you in this work. Of course, you can just celebrate with your own students. Even if you celebrate with only your students, you can choose to make the celebration "bigger," or more special, by doing it in the media center, auditorium, or even outside—if the weather permits. If it's preferable and more enjoyable, however, for you and your students to hold the celebration in your classroom, then that's what you should do. You can still make it special. What you do at this celebration will be up to you and your students.
- **Plan an Authors' Tea:** Each student can read aloud a piece of writing. The celebration could just be for your class, or you could invite others to join, such as family members and those in the school community. You can decorate your classroom and have some goodies to share. (Generally, food accompanies a celebration!) To do this on a smaller scale, you could have students share their work in small groups, instead of to a larger audience, or you could have them read, one-on-one or in small groups, to students in a different grade.
- **Share Goals and Accomplishments:** Though students will reflect on their goals independently, it could be a worthwhile activity to share this reflection more widely. It's interesting for students to hear what their classmates achieved, and it will be rewarding for them to have their classmates clap and cheer for their successes.

- **Write a Letter:** A great way for students to celebrate is to write about all they've achieved. They can write a letter to themselves, to you, or to a family member. You'll need to guide them through this process, and the sample lesson plan in this chapter will provide suggestions for how to do this. If you choose this option, make sure this isn't your only celebration, as most students will not view writing a letter as a celebration. Also, this is a solitary activity, and the end of year calls for an opportunity to celebrate with others. Students may choose to share an excerpt from this letter if you do a class sharing of goals. Though students may not necessarily consider writing a letter to be a celebration, when they read it later—maybe even many years later—they will feel proud, and it may cause them to smile with fond remembrance or even shed a tear of joy.

TAKEAWAYS

It may be difficult for students to determine exactly what they will take away from this year-long goal-setting process. The best way to reflect upon this experience and decide on takeaways might be to provide students with some question prompts like the ones below. You can ask students to respond to three or four questions, or share their takeaways in another way.

- What is your greatest success from this year? How did your goals help you achieve it?
- What's an area where you wish you'd achieved more? How might you have made greater progress?
- What's the most important lesson you learned?
- What's your greatest achievement outside of writing? Did you create a goal that helped you achieve it?
- What do you most want to continue next year, and why?
- What will you leave behind, and why?
- What did you learn about yourself through this goal-setting process?

MOVING FORWARD

It would be a shame to have done all of this work and made all of this progress and not have a plan for continuing this goal-setting journey. Moving forward is an integral part of this process. In fact, the whole idea of goal setting is that we are constantly keeping our eyes on the horizon. Whether we achieve our goals or fall short, we are reflecting, adjusting, and making new plans that keep us looking to the future. As with takeaways, students may not know exactly how to do this "moving forward" work on their own, so perhaps you can provide a list of what they might do to continue the work, even if their teacher next year doesn't require them to set goals. They should then pick one or two of the choices on the list below—or one of their own—that they know will motivate them.

- Write your new goals based on your progress toward this year's goals and what you'd like to carry forward.
- Make a commitment to continue meeting with your accountability partner. Make sure your accountability partner knows that you'd like to continue to meet and agrees to offer this support. If not, you'll need to find a new partner. Put a date on both of your calendars for the first time that you'll meet with your partner to discuss your goals. You can choose the next date at your first meeting.
- Write dates on your calendar, not only for when you will meet with your accountability partner but also for when you will check in on your progress, reflect on your goals, and revise them.
- Since your goals in this class focused primarily on writing, set some goals in other areas of your life.
- Pick something you'd like to learn more about that can help you with a goal, and create a goal to learn about it. (For example, even though I've put the goal "on hold" for now, when I wanted to learn more about middle grade books, I read several of them and joined a group for those either currently writing or interested in writing this genre.)

In the spirit of moving forward and taking our goals with us, teacher Betsy Hubbard asks her students to set aspirational but realistic goals for the summer break. Her students make small posters, "listing two-three goals they have for themselves as writers" (Hubbard 2017).

> *Our summer goals will be what they [students] feel they are independently capable of practicing with success. It might be, always using punctuation or remembering to organize using paragraphs and structure. Maybe their goals will be to continue to write catchy leads or informative pieces that include voice and personal stories (Hubbard 2017).*

As her students finish their summer goal posters, Hubbard encourages them to place visual reminders of their goals in places where they will see them often—such as on the refrigerator or inside a special notebook.

Whether you focus on guiding students toward their next steps in the more immediate future (like summer break), the longer term future (next school year or future years), or a little of both, helping students plan for the ways they will continue to set and work toward goals when you are no longer their teacher is one last gift you can give them.

SAMPLE LESSON: WRITING AN END-OF-YEAR LETTER TO CELEBRATE AND MOVE FORWARD

Note: I wasn't sure about including a sample lesson in this chapter because I'm confident that with all of the samples I've provided in the preceding chapters, you'll be able to create your own—as I know you've been planning your own lessons throughout this process anyway. You can certainly draw from lessons on monitoring and revising goals in Chapters 6 and 7 to help with end-of-year reflection, but you might also want to focus on celebrations. Here I share a lesson that provides end-of-year closure and space for students to reflect upon what they've learned and how they can continue this work in the future.

Model You may want to start the lesson by sharing a letter you've written to yourself about your goals this year, or an excerpt of one. You'll also want to give students guidelines (such as the ones in Figure 8.1 (Appendix M)), or perhaps a checklist, for what they might mention in their letter. For example, they could start by listing each of their goals and describing the progress they made. As usual, students should give examples of evidence of their progress. Students can also share how they will celebrate, what they've taken away from the goal-setting experience, and what they plan to do next. In your model, you should consider touching on each of these requirements.

At this time, you should let students know that they can decide if they would like to address their letter to you, a family member, or themselves. Also, though I've set up this lesson as writing a letter, you can allow students to use bullet points or even create a graphic which responds to the requirements. Depending upon your expectations, the model you share may be done using one of these formats.

End-of-Year Goal Reflection Letter Guidelines

You have worked on self-selected writing goals throughout the year to improve your writing. Now it's time to write a letter to celebrate and close out this process. Use this opportunity to reflect upon all the progress you've made and what you can continue to do to be a successful writer as well as what areas might still need your focus.

After you have written your letter, compare it to the list of "Required Elements" below to make sure you've written a thorough letter. **Your letter must contain *specific examples from your writing* to support the points in your letter.** Of course, ***proofread and edit*** your letter carefully.

REQUIRED ELEMENTS

- ***Date and Salutation*** Date your letter. Your letter should be addressed to: "Dear ______________, [Write your name, your teacher's name, a caregiver's name, or the name of someone else you'd like to read your letter]."
- ***Introduction*** Start with an exciting lead to draw the reader into your letter. What do you want the reader to be aware of while reading your letter?
- ***Explanation and Evidence of Goals*** What were your writing goals this year? Why did you choose them, and what strategies were helpful in working on/achieving your goals?
- ***Improvement/Growth as a Writer*** How have you become a better writer this year? Be sure to include examples/quotes from your own writing and reflections to support your opinion. What particular class lessons and assignments helped you? What initiative(s) did you take to improve your writing?
- ***Next Steps*** What writing goals would you like to continue or add next year? What strategies will you use to achieve your goals and to continue your growth as a writer?
- ***Conclusion*** What final reflections/thoughts do you want to share about yourself as a writer and the goal-setting process? Conclude your letter on a positive, inviting note that makes the reader want to cheer for you. Remember to sign your letter.

FIGURE 8.1 End-of-Year Goal Reflection Letter Guidelines

Respond Ask students how they feel about reflecting on their goals at the end of the year and what they think they'll highlight in their letter or graphic. They may share their thoughts with a partner, in small groups, or with the whole class.

Try It Students should take out their goals and goal-setting artifacts (written assignments, assessments, reflections, etc.). They should decide where they want to start. Do they want to start with celebrations or takeaways? They may write a sentence about a celebration they'll plan, or they may quickly sketch a graphic which shows a takeaway.

Questions Ask students if they have any questions. If you've given students a choice about writing a letter or creating a graphic, you could ask students to raise their hands to show which option they plan to do. It could be interesting for you and the students to see who plans to do what.

Do It If your students have recently revised and reflected upon their goals, they should use the Goal Revision Organizer (Figure 7.1) as a support for writing their letter. If they haven't recently done this work, then they should review their goals and strategies, going through the process of determining the category for each goal (accomplished, unsuccessful, or more-to-do), and thinking about how to carry these goals into the future. They should fill out a fresh copy of the Goal Revision Organizer as they work. Students will likely need more than one day to complete this task.

Share Ask students to share an excerpt from their letter or graphic with a classmate. You may then call on a few students to share with the whole class.

Reflect Ask students to reflect upon the following questions. Were there any surprises? What part of the assignment will they work on next? Will they check in on goals they've set in other parts of their life?

REFLECT AND SET YOUR OWN GOALS

Think about what you've learned about goal setting this year and what your students have taught you.

- What will you do differently next year to guide your students toward success with their goals?
- What will you do differently next year to achieve success with your own goals?
- Will you reflect on your own goals before the school year ends, along with your students, or do you need the school year to end before you do your own reflection? (If it's the latter, make sure you do it!)

Set a goal for how you will ensure that there's time for you and your students to wrap up their goals at the end of the year and move forward.

Since there's so much that happens at the end of the school year, when is it best to build in time for students to reflect on their goals? Make sure you set aside time for celebrations, too!

Examples:

1. I will write dates on my calendar for when students will reflect upon their goals and how and when we will celebrate.
2. I will plan for a class share during which students will explain what they learned about setting goals and how they will move forward and use these skills next school year—whether or not they have a teacher who will work on a goal-setting process with them.
3. I will write dates on my calendar for when I will reflect upon my own goals and how and when I will celebrate. Part of my celebration will include sharing this process—and this book—with another teacher to encourage that person to engage in goal setting with their students.

FINAL THOUGHTS

I hope you've enjoyed engaging in this goal-setting process with your students and witnessed the growth they've made as a result. I also hope you've made growth with your own goals, too, and are feeling satisfied with what you've accomplished. Even if you didn't achieve all of your goals, if you were successful in guiding your students through this process, then kudos to you!

As you wrap up the year, please encourage your students to continue to set goals in other aspects of their academic and personal lives, even if a teacher, coach, or another adult doesn't require them to do so. I want your students to become independent learners who think critically and creatively, ask questions, collaborate with peers, direct their own learning, and are willing to put time and effort into revising their writing to make it the best it can be and into revising their goals to achieve optimum success.

My greatest hope for you and your students is that this work will bring you a sense of pride in your achievements, the motivation to keep making progress, and the realization that you have agency over what you desire to accomplish—in school and in life. Now go forth and set goals!

APPENDIX A

Goal Setting Organizer

Name: ______________________________ Date: ___________

Choose **THREE** goals to work on in all of your written assignments. Write them down in simple statements. Please select **TWO** goals for writing (content/quality) and **ONE** goal for editing.

After you have chosen your goals, select strategies you will use to achieve them. You must write at least **TWO** strategies for each goal.

MY WRITING GOAL	STRATEGIES/HOW I WILL WORK TOWARD MY GOAL
Example: I will work on organizing my thoughts and ideas in my writing.	1. I will carefully plan my writing before I begin to write. 2. I will work on my transitions from one thought/idea to the next so that my writing flows in a logical way.

APPENDIX B

Goal Setting Organizer with Check-in Dates

Name: ______________________________ Date: ___________

Choose **THREE** goals to work on in all of your written assignments. Write them down in simple statements. Please select **TWO** goals for writing (content/quality) and **ONE** goal for editing.

After you have chosen your goals, select strategies you will use to achieve them. You must write at least **TWO** strategies for each goal.

Date of First Check-in Toward Progress:
Date of Second Check-in Toward Progress:
Date of Third Check-in Toward Progress:
Date of Final Check-in Toward Progress:

MY WRITING GOALS	STRATEGIES/HOW I WILL WORK TOWARD MY GOAL
Example: I will work on organizing my thoughts and ideas in my writing.	1. I will carefully plan my writing before I begin to write. 2. I will work on my transitions from one thought/idea to the next so that my writing flows in a logical way.

APPENDIX C

Accountability Partner Guidelines

Teacher note: As you get started with accountability partners, you may want to make copies of this chart for students to use to guide their first meetings. Two copies are provided here so that each partner can have a copy. Students may even want to keep this chart in their notebooks or have a digital copy to refer to each time they meet with their partner.

ACCOUNTABILITY PARTNERS SUPPORT EACH OTHER'S GOALS

Here are some ways to check in with your partner.

- How's your goal coming along?
- What strategies are you working on right now?
- When do you plan to finish this?
- Is there anything I can help you with?
- When should we check in on this again?

ACCOUNTABILITY PARTNERS SUPPORT EACH OTHER'S GOALS

Here are some ways to check in with your partner.

- How's your goal coming along?
- What strategies are you working on right now?
- When do you plan to finish this?
- Is there anything I can help you with?
- When should we check in on this again?

APPENDIX D

Accountability Partner Recording Sheet

After listening to your partner, write one to two sentences describing your partner's goal and plan for moving toward it. After writing these sentences, check in with your partner: "Did I write your goal and plan correctly?" Then, your partner will do the same for you.

Partners' names: ____

Today's meeting date: _______________

_______________'s goal/plan:

____

____

____

_______________'s goal/plan:

____

____

____

Our next meeting will be _______________ (date).

APPENDIX E

How to Give and Receive Peer Feedback

When giving peer feedback:

- Listen to your partner.
- Ask, "What would you like feedback on today?"
- Give your partner specific feedback.
- Encourage and celebrate your partner's work.

When receiving peer feedback:

- Come ready to share.
- After sharing, say, "I'm ready for your feedback on [name something specific]."
- Listen to the feedback.
- If you don't understand part of the feedback, say, "Can you explain what you mean by [name point of confusion]?"
- Say, "Thank you for your feedback. I am going to try [name a suggestion your partner has given]."

APPENDIX F

Peer Feedback Form

Name: ______________________________ Date: __________

(Fill out before peer conversation.)

Today I want feedback on ____

____

____

(Fill out during/after conversation.)

An idea from my partner that I'm going to try is _______________________

____

____

APPENDIX G

Praise/Polish/Question Peer Feedback Form

Name: ______________________________ Date: ___________

This feedback is for _______________________ (partner's name).

I am giving feedback on ____

____

(name writing assignment and goal).

Praise ____

____

____

Polish ____

____

____

Question (Optional) ____

____

____

APPENDIX H

Ways to Give Your Partner Critical Feedback

- What would happen if…?
- Have you considered…?
- Are there other ways you might…?

APPENDIX I

Feedback Implementation Planning Form

Name: ______________________________ Date: ___________

My goal:

____

____

____

What feedback have I received on this assignment?

____

____

____

____

Have I received any similar or related feedback on previous assignments?

____

____

What feedback will I implement in this assignment?

____

____

____

What feedback will I implement first?

____

____

What feedback will I save for another time or choose not to implement?

____

____

APPENDIX J

Goal Monitoring Form

Name: ______________________________ Date: ___________

Goal 1:

Progress I've Made Toward My Goal

____

____

Evidence (List at least three pieces of evidence from your writing.)

1. ____

   ____

2. ____

   ____

3. ____

   ____

Next Steps/What I Want to Continue to Do/Something New I Will Do

____

____

Goal 2:

Progress I've Made Toward My Goal

____

____

Evidence (List at least three pieces of evidence from your writing.)

1. ____
   ____
2. ____
   ____
3. ____
   ____

Next Steps/What I Want to Continue to Do/Something New I Will Do

____

____

Goal 3:

Progress I've Made Toward My Goal

____

____

Evidence (List at least three pieces of evidence from your writing.)

1. ____
   ____
2. ____
   ____
3. ____
   ____

Next Steps/What I Want to Continue to Do/Something New I Will Do

____

____

APPENDIX K

Ways to Help a Classmate Monitor Goals

- "Where did you find evidence of working toward your goal?"
- "One way I notice you working toward your goal is [name evidence]."
- "Will you continue to work on this goal in this unit, or will you set a new goal?"

APPENDIX L

Goal Revision Organizer

Name: ______________________________ Date: ___________

Revising our goals is an important part of the goal-setting process and can help us make greater progress toward achieving our goals. As you reflect upon your progress, use this organizer to determine the status of your goals, what revisions you'll make, and your next steps.

MY WRITING GOAL	STRATEGIES/ HOW I WILL WORK TOWARD MY GOAL	GOAL STATUS (CHECK ONE)	WHAT I'LL DO NEXT (CHECK ONE)	PLAN FOR MOVING FORWARD (WRITE A NEW/REVISED GOAL, NEW STRATEGIES, ETC.)
		☐ Accomplished ☐ Unsuccessful ☐ More-to-do	☐ I will set a new goal. ☐ I will abandon this goal. ☐ I will revise this goal. ☐ I will revise one or more strategies.	
		☐ Accomplished ☐ Unsuccessful ☐ More-to-do	☐ I will set a new goal. ☐ I will abandon this goal. ☐ I will revise this goal. ☐ I will revise one or more strategies.	
		☐ Accomplished ☐ Unsuccessful ☐ More-to-do	☐ I will set a new goal. ☐ I will abandon this goal. ☐ I will revise this goal. ☐ I will revise one or more strategies.	

APPENDIX M

End-of-Year Goal Reflection Letter Guidelines

You have worked on self-selected writing goals throughout the year to improve your writing. Now it's time to write a letter to celebrate and close out this process. Use this opportunity to reflect upon all the progress you've made and what you can continue to do to be a successful writer as well as what areas might still need your focus.

After you have written your letter, compare it to the list of "Required Elements" below to make sure you've written a thorough letter. **Your letter must contain *specific examples from your writing* to support the points in your letter.** Of course, ***proofread and edit*** your letter carefully.

REQUIRED ELEMENTS

- ***Date and Salutation*** Date your letter. Your letter should be addressed to: "Dear ______________, [Write your name, your teacher's name, a caregiver's name, or the name of someone else you'd like to read your letter]."
- ***Introduction*** Start with an exciting lead to draw the reader into your letter. What do you want the reader to be aware of while reading your letter?
- ***Explanation and Evidence of Goals*** What were your writing goals this year? Why did you choose them, and what strategies were helpful in working on/achieving your goals?
- ***Improvement/Growth as a Writer*** How have you become a better writer this year? Be sure to include examples/quotes from your own writing and reflections to support your opinion. What particular class lessons and assignments helped you? What initiative(s) did you take to improve your writing?
- ***Next Steps*** What writing goals would you like to continue or add next year? What strategies will you use to achieve your goals and to continue your growth as a writer?
- ***Conclusion*** What final reflections/thoughts do you want to share about yourself as a writer and the goal-setting process? Conclude your letter on a positive, inviting note that makes the reader want to cheer for you. Remember to sign your letter.

APPENDIX N

Goal Setting Process Ladder

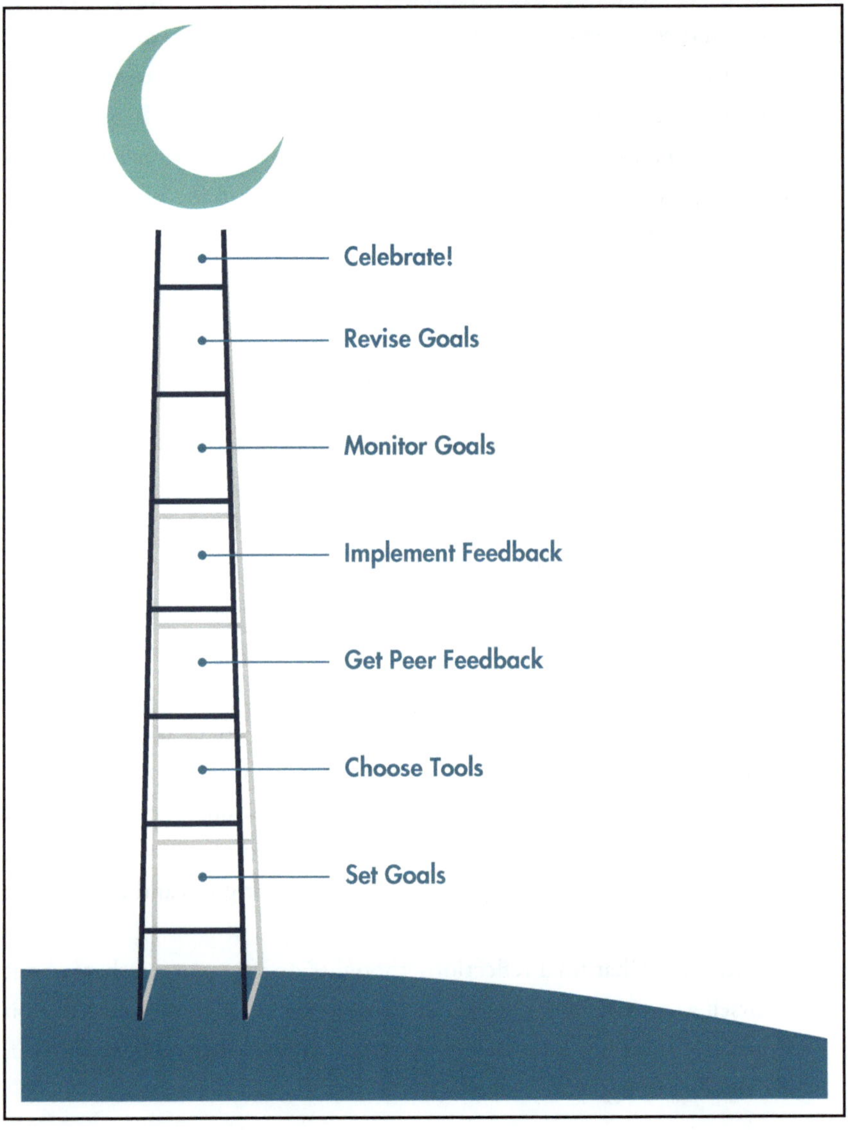

REFERENCES

Ayres, Ruth. 2013. *Celebrating Writers: From Possibilities through Publication*. Portsmouth, NH: Stenhouse.

Brookhart, Susan M. 2008. *How To Give Effective Feedback to Your Students*. Alexandria, VA: ASCD.

Carroll, Jaquelin H. and Charlene Noelani-Kahuanui Christenson. 1995. "Teaching and Learning about Student Goal Setting in a Fifth-Grade Classroom." *Language Arts* 72 (1): 42–9.

Ferlazzo, Larry. 2017. "Response: Provide 'Voice' and 'Choice' When Students Set Goals." *Education Week,* January 17. https://www.edweek.org/teaching-learning/opinion-response-provide-voice-and-choice-when-students-set-goals/2017/01.

Fisher, Douglas, Nancy Frey, Sarah Ortega, and John Hattie. 2023. *Teaching Students to Drive Their Learning: A Playbook on Engagement and Self-Regulation*. Thousand Oaks, CA: Corwin.

Hubbard, Betsy. 2016. "Students and Goal Setting: My Choice, My Growth, My Responsibility." *Two Writing Teachers,* October 9. https://twowritingteachers.org/2016/10/09/students-and-goal-setting/.

Hubbard, Betsy. 2017. "The Why, The Slide, and Goal Setting: Keep Learning Going Throughout the Summer." *Two Writing Teachers,* May 1. https://twowritingteachers.org/2017/05/01/summer-slide-goal-setting/.

Nordengren, Chase. 2022. *Step Into Student Goal Setting: A Path to Growth, Motivation and Agency*. Thousand Oaks, CA: Corwin.

Serravallo, Jennifer. 2017. *The Writing Strategies Book: Your Everything Guide to Developing Skilled Writers*. Portsmouth, NH: Heinemann.

Toro, Stephanie. 2021. "Guiding Students to Set Academic Goals." *Edutopia,* October 12. https://www.edutopia.org/article/guiding-students-set-academic-goals/.

For Product Safety Concerns and Information,
please contact our EU representative GPSR@taylorandfrancis.com
Taylor & Francis Verlag GmbH, Kaufingerstraße 24,
80331 München, Germany

Printed by Integrated Books International,
United States of America